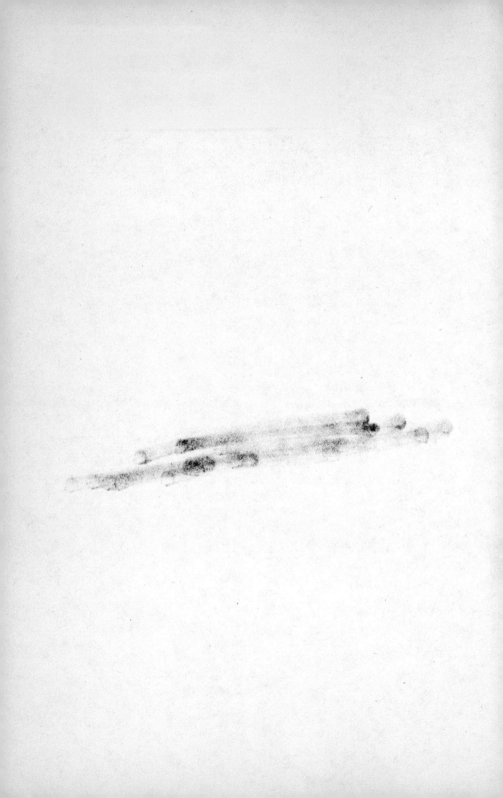

Aggression and Crimes of Violence

Aggression and Crimes of Violence

Second Edition

Jeffrey H. Goldstein

Temple University

New York   Oxford
OXFORD UNIVERSITY PRESS
1986

Oxford University Press

Oxford New York Toronto
Delhi Bombay Calcutta Madras Karachi
Petaling Jaya Singapore Hong Kong Tokyo
Nairobi Dar es Salaam Cape Town
Melbourne Auckland

and associated companies in
Beirut Berlin Ibadan Nicosia

Published by Oxford University Press, Inc.,
200 Madison Avenue, New York, New York 10016

Oxford is a registered trademark of Oxford University Press

Library of Congress Cataloging-in-Publication Data

Goldstein, Jeffrey H.
  Aggression and crimes of violence.

  Bibliography: p.
  Includes index.
  1. Violence—United States. 2. Aggressiveness
(Psychology) 3. Crime and criminals—United States.
I. Title.
HN90.V5G65 1986   364.2   85-28520
  ISBN 0-19-503943-2
  ISBN 0-19-503944-0 (pbk.)

9 8 7 6 5 4 3 2 1
Printed in the United States of America
on acid-free paper

To the memory of my father, Robert

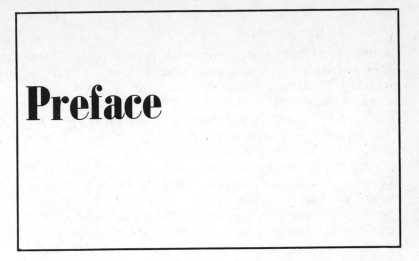

Preface

Aggression is arguably the most serious of human problems. The quality of family life is threatened by violence against wives and children, the attractiveness of America's cities is marred by street crime, and the human species as a whole is threatened by the specter of nuclear annihilation. What do we know and what do we believe—the two are hardly the same—about the human propensity for violence? What can be done about violence based on what we know?

Aggression and Crimes of Violence is designed to explore the empirical evidence with respect to human aggression and violent crime. Based on this review, implications for the control and elimination of violence are drawn. Others might see the implications differently for there is no systematic way to infer policy from research. I doubt that public policy should be based only on psychological (or any other) empirical research. However, I believe that public policy should, at the very least, not be inconsistent with what we have learned about human behavior.

The literature summarized in this book comes from a variety

of disciplines: anthropology, criminology, education, law, medicine, physiology, political science, psychiatry, psychology, and sociology. Since these fields often use technical language and concepts that do not translate easily from one specialty to another, a simple model of aggression is introduced in Chapter 1 that will provide a common language with which to evaluate and integrate these various approaches.

Although the concept of aggression is examined critically in Chapter 1, a definition is in order here. Aggression is *behavior whose intent is the physical or psychological injury of another person.* Given this definition, not only hitting someone but also embarrassing another person is considered aggressive. Intentionally depriving another unnecessarily of a valued resource, such as a job, would also be aggressive. Obviously the crimes of homicide, assault, and rape are acts of aggression, but so too are the not illegal acts of spanking a child, name-calling, and nearly all forms of prejudice and discrimination. Excluded from this conception of aggression are the accidental or unintentional injury of others as well as behavior that, in popular parlance, is labeled aggressive simply because of its persistence or vigor, as in the term "aggressive salesman." Self-assertion is nonaggressive unless it is also designed to injure another. The destruction of objects, such as smashing a vase against a wall, is likewise excluded from this conception of aggression because it does not involve injury of another human being. While it is possible to make a distinction between *violence,* the physical injury of others, and *aggression,* the psychological injury of others, the two terms are used interchangeably here. Although this definition of aggression will serve our purposes adequately, there are some difficulties associated with it. For example, some behaviors are not clearly aggressive or nonaggressive (such as euthanasia and abortion), and it is not always easy or possible to determine what a person's intentions were (see Kaufmann, 1970; Mummendey, 1984; Siann, 1985; Tedeschi, Smith, & Brown, 1974; Zillmann, 1979).

Aggression might best be viewed as a continuum on which any behavior might fall depending upon how much "aggressiveness" it contains. At one end of the continuum would be behavior that has neither hostile intention nor effect. A behavior with no hostile intention but which nevertheless injures another would also fall toward the nonaggressive pole, according to our definition. An act designed to injure or kill another person would anchor the extreme aggressive end of the continuum. Aggression and crime, however, are behaviors that are "overdetermined"—that is, they tend not to be acts of a purely violent or illegal nature, but serve additional purposes for the offender, among others. Most behaviors of concern to us in this book contain both aggressive and nonaggressive components. Spanking a child to "teach him a lesson" is a common example of such a mixed motive. *Instrumental aggression* is the term used by psychologists to refer to behavior that has both injurious and noninjurious goals. One of the main contentions of this book is that aggressive behavior used to achieve a personal goal, such as wealth or power, and which may be perceived by the actor as justified (or even as nonaggressive), is a primary cause of the aggressive and criminal behavior of others.

This revision of *Aggression and Crimes of Violence* not only updates the literature reviewed in the first edition, but contains new and expanded discussions of contemporary research topics, including predicting dangerousness, family violence, the effects of pornography on aggression, research on sports violence, and the psychology of war and peace.

I have tried to write in a manner accessible to readers with no formal training in research methods or statistics. In order to present a concise summary of the bases of and possible solutions to crime and aggression, it has been necessary in some places to simplify the often complex and not entirely consistent research literature. Where inconsistencies in the literature exist, I have usually pointed them out. In other places, it has been necessary to fill gaps in our knowledge with hypothetical analyses that are subject to future test. I can only hope that these speculations will not be misconstrued as statements of fact.

St. Davids, Pennsylvania   J.H.G.
April 1986

Acknowledgments

Aggression and Crimes of Violence was originally published as part of the Oxford University Press Reconstruction of Society Series edited by Robert E. Lana and Ralph L. Rosnow. I am grateful to them for their continued assistance with this book. The first edition benefited from the support and guidance of many friends and colleagues. My greatest debt is to Frank Winer, who read and commented on the entire manuscript. The advice and suggestions of James Averill, Ronald Baenninger, Helene Feinberg, Robert Feinberg, James Hurley, David Kipnis, George Levinger, Ashley Montagu, Jack Rakosky, and Harriet Serenkin are gratefully acknowledged. Many of them commented on parts of the revision as well. Portions of the book were written with support from Temple University and a National Science Foundation grant to the Department of Psychology, University of Massachusetts, Amherst.

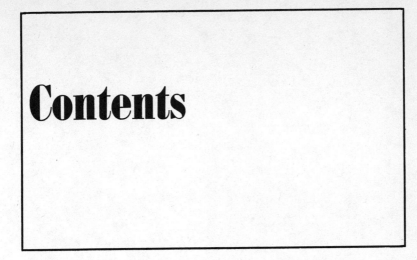

Contents

Aggression and Crimes of Violence

1
The Nature of Human Aggression

What we believe about aggression determines what we do about it. Below are some prevalent beliefs about human aggression.

1. Failure to express anger results in heart disease, stress, and high blood pressure.
2. Humans are instinctively aggressive. Safe, acceptable channels for the expression of this destructive instinct must be found or society as a whole will suffer.
3. The aggressive instinct can be controlled through substitute activities, such as football games and Clint Eastwood movies. These enable us to rid ourselves vicariously of the urge to commit mayhem.
4. Children should be allowed to play aggressively. This will "get it out of their system" and they will be better behaved as a result.
5. Child and spouse abuse are usually committed by people who are mentally ill.
6. Violent crime is a result of the aggressive instinct. In some individuals and groups this instinct is abnormally strong.

These individuals are responsible for the majority of violent crimes.

7. It is a biological fact that men are more aggressive than women.

8. Emotions are physiological reactions that "just happen" to you, so there's nothing you can do about them. Because anger is an emotion, it cannot be controlled.

9. People become aggressive when they are angry. Anger fuels aggression. Expressing anger is a healthy way of dealing with it; it also makes you feel better.

10. War is one expression of the aggression instinct. It is unavoidable because humans have an inborn need to satisfy their aggressive urges. Peace is an aberration, a temporary period between wars.

These statements constitute what I call *the 10 myths of aggression*. They are widely believed, and they are all false. These 10 myths form the basis for many of our beliefs about human violence and crime. They also color our efforts to deal with violence at home, with crime in the streets, and with policy toward other countries. To the extent that our dealings with others are based on these beliefs, our actions are apt to prove ineffective and, in some instances, to produce the very conditions they are designed to ameliorate.

Is Aggression an Instinct?

Throughout modern history the answer to the question of whether aggression in humans is innate or learned has swung first one way, then the other. Because at various times the answer to the question has changed, there exist in our social and legal systems methods and remedies for the reduction and control of violence that are not necessarily consistent with one another nor with current scientific thinking on the issue. The point is not that scientific thinking changes over time—it should and does change as new information and perspectives are acquired—but that the formal and informal policies and controls used to reduce aggression are influenced by how we conceive of aggression.

In recent years people's beliefs about the bases of human aggression have leaned toward an instinctual bias. This is due largely to four influences: (1) the accounts of aggression by ethologists and sociobiologists, such as Konrad Lorenz (1966), Desmond Morris (1967), and E. O. Wilson (1975; Lumsden & Wilson, 1981); (2) the popularity and pervasiveness of Freudian theory (1930); (3) the dramatic research on electrical and chemical stimulation of the brain (Delgado, 1967, 1969); and (4) the biological emphasis in the mass media's presentation of violence (Goldstein, 1986a).

So-So Biology: One Giant Leap Toward Mankind

The ethological arguments proposed by Lorenz, Morris, and Wilson can be summarized by saying that there is ample evidence that our animal ancestors were instinctively violent beings, and since we have evolved from them, we too must be the bearers of destructive impulses in our genetic makeup. Lorenz (1964) states "There cannot be any doubt, in the opinion of any biologically minded scientist, that intraspecific aggression is, in man, just as much of a spontaneous instinctive drive as in most other higher vertebrates" (p. 49).

In his book, *On Aggression,* Lorenz (1966) argues that while humans and animals share an instinct for aggressive behavior, humans, unlike other species, lack a well-developed mechanism for the *inhibition* of aggression. Many species of animal inhibit aggression in response to the visible and audible pain and suffering of their victims. Human technology has made possible the infliction of injury and death at distances too great to enable perception of these "pain cues," so we humans do not inhibit our aggression at the sound and sight of our enemies' suffering.

There are essentially two difficulties with these arguments. First, the evidence that animals, at least the higher primates, are instinctively aggressive is not very convincing. Alland

(1972), Barnett (1983), Binford (1972), and others (e.g., Kim, 1976; Montagu, 1968; Schneirla, 1968) have examined the evidence and found it wanting. Second, even if the evidence reviewed by the ethologists and sociobiologists were sufficient to establish that infrahuman species were innately violent, we would still have to ask whether that proves humans are prone to aggression. Of course, it does not. The *likelihood* that humans are instinctively aggressive would be increased if some primate species were shown to be aggressive, but we would still have to entertain the possibility that *Homo sapiens,* with unique genes of its own, was not a violent species.

There is not much doubt that humans *can* behave like phylogenetically inferior species. There is no reason why an organism with a complex nervous system, such as ours, cannot behave like or mimic the behavior of animals with less complex nervous systems. However, to argue that because we *can* behave like lower organisms, we *must* behave like them is preposterous. If we take learning experiments on animals, such as operant conditioning studies in which an organism is rewarded for performing a certain response, there is no neurological or psychological reason why a human being cannot also learn responses in this way. To argue that this is the way humans learn—simply because it is one way in which they may learn—begs the question. It is obviously true that humans can and do learn behaviors through operant conditioning. However, to preclude other uniquely human ways of learning is a serious shortcoming of much contemporary psychology. Likewise, to argue that humans learn aggression in the same ways that other species learn aggression (if indeed it is learned in other species) is to ignore the possibility that there are species-specific aggressions in people or that there are specifically human routes to learning and behaving.

Monkeying Around in the Brains of Primates

Research on brain physiology and chemistry, particularly that on electrical and chemical stimulation of the brain, has demonstrated that it is possible in many instances to make normally docile animals—and humans—extraordinarily violent. The best known work in this field has been done by José Delgado (1969). By implanting sensitive radio receivers in the brains of cats, monkeys, and other species, Delgado has been able to control the aggressive behavior of his research subjects by activating various parts of the limbic system, particularly the hypothalamus. Heath (1963) has reported a similar ability to control aggression in humans.

What implications does this dramatic research hold for an understanding of, and ability to control, human aggression? First, and perhaps most important, is the frightening possibility that human aggressiveness could be controlled by others against the actor's will. Electrodes could be implanted in infants' brains at birth, or in adults' during routine operations, without the knowledge or consent of the recipients. Aggression could then be fairly reliably controlled by the possessor of the appropriate radio transmitter. Both Moyer (1971a) and Clark (1971) have made eloquent appeals that such technological abilities not be used for antisocial purposes, if indeed they are used at all.

In many of the brain stimulation studies on aggression, it has been reported that, even when stimulated, some animals will not engage in aggression unless certain environmental features are present, such as an "appropriate" target for attack (Delgado, 1967). For example, if the only available target of aggression is an animal more dominant than the one stimulated, no attack will occur. Only when the target is inferior in status will electrical stimulation result in attack (Delgado, 1969; Flynn, 1967). Thus, even with infrahumans, brain stimulation does not guarantee that aggression will ensue, a finding which calls into question the notion that aggression is purely a matter of brain chemistry and physiology, as some have argued (Mark & Ervin, 1970). Let us suppose, however, that the research discussed here was even more conclusive, that by stimulating the brain's lateral hypothalamus aggression could be uniformly and consistently elicited from humans as well as from animals. The evidence is far from this reliable, but if it were, what would this mean insofar as our ability to understand, predict, and control human aggression was concerned? My own conclusion would be that it has very little demonstrable relevance. While the brain stimulation research has now been conducted in a sufficient number of circumstances to prove of some generality, it says nothing about how the brain is stimulated *in vivo*. What are those variables that cause the lateral hypothalamus to be stimulated when an organism's skull remains intact? One answer, of course, is that changes in body chemistry are likely to suppress or activate different parts of the limbic system, but the question of just what influences which hormones to stimulate the hypothalamus remains largely unexplored. It is likely that changes in body chemistry result from stimuli outside the person, in his or her environment, and from affect-laden thoughts of the individual. We will have to look outside the corporeal package, then, in order to answer this question satisfactorily.

As with research on infrahuman species, physiological research can provide us with valuable information about the nature of aggression mechanisms. It has instructed us within a very short period of time and within fairly narrow limits which internal structures are likely to be implicated in aggressive behavior. However, physiology is only one part of the complex problem of aggression. That aggression is a physical act there can be no doubt, and that brain physiology and chemistry are involved in aggressive behavior is equally clear. Environmental, cognitive, and social factors, though, are also implicated in the physiological research (Wilson & Herrnstein, 1985). Stimulation of parts of the brain does not guarantee that aggressive behavior will ensue, and, further, it is likely that in natural situations (i.e., those of nonintervention in the brain) it is cognitive and environmental factors that are themselves responsible for the stimulation in the first place. It is also conceivable that those portions of the brain found during surgical intervention to elicit aggression are not those involved in nonintervention situations.

Though this is an unlikely possibility, it does serve to point out the difficulties in generalizing from a contrived to a natural situation.

Genes and the Genesis of Aggression

Those who wish to make the case that aggression is biologically caused often attach their arguments to a particular finding that becomes faddish. At the turn of the century, criminals were believed to be of a certain physiological "type." The criminologist Cesare Lombroso wrote:

> The criminal by nature has a feeble cranial capacity, a heavy and developed jaw, projecting (eye) ridges, an abnormal and asymmetrical cranium . . . projecting ears, frequently a crooked or flat nose. Criminals are subject to color blindness; lefthandedness is common; their muscular force is feeble. (quoted in S. Chorover, 1979, pp. 179–180)

This is the forerunner of today's belief in criminal chromosomes. In arguing that criminality could be predicted from physiognomy, a "rational criminology" became possible. In the late 1960s and 1970s the belief that hyperaggressiveness in males was caused by a genetic abnormality was widespread. It had been reported that males imprisoned for violent offenses were more likely to have an extra Y chromosome, the so-called "XYY males." The normal male has, as one of his 23 pairs of chromosomes, one pair that determines sex characteristics, an X and a Y chromosome. The normal female has two X chromosomes. The incidence of XYY males in the general population is approximately 1 in 3,000. Jacobs, Brunton, and Melville (1965) reported that approximately 3 percent of the men in maximum security prisons and hospitals for the "criminally insane" in Edinburgh were XYYs. Subsequent studies and critiques have cast doubt on the importance of the additional Y chromosome in criminality (Jarvik, Klodin, & Matsuyama, 1973; Montagu, 1968). Of course, the additional Y chromosome could not be a primary determinant of crime since over

97 percent of those incarcerated for violence were not XYY males. Second, it was not clear what proportion of XYY males did not show signs of antisocial conduct. Furthermore, intelligence was likely to mediate the relationship between genes and crime in that the least intelligent men were apt to be caught and convicted (Witkin et al., 1976). Montagu (1968) pointed out that the XYY phenomenon is not a syndrome that reliably leads to particular behaviors, but an anomaly that, depending on environmental conditions, may lead to a host of possible behaviors.

For decades, paleo-anthropologists and biologists believed that stone artifacts found with ancient humanoid skeletal remains were destructive weapons. The existence of such "weapons" was taken as evidence of our early ancestors' innate aggressiveness (see Ardrey, 1961, 1966). However, within the last few years, some anthropologists have found it more plausible to believe that these objects were not weapons at all but tools used to scavenge for food (Cordes, 1984; Hammond, 1984; Rensberger, 1984).

Freudian Slips

Following the horrors of World War I, Freud proposed that humans possess a death instinct, Thanatos. He suggested that societies had to learn to control the expression of both the life and death instincts. Thus are developed the social mores and rules regulating sexual and aggressive conduct.

Contemporary psychoanalytic theorists, building more or less on Freud's own work, have retained the notion that aggression is an instinctive drive (Stepansky, 1977). Common in current psychoanalytic thinking is the notion that aggression must be discharged periodically lest it build up to such a point that its expression becomes spontaneous and uncontrollable. Zinberg and Fellman (1967) go so far as to suggest that war itself serves to discharge the aggression instinct not only for participants but for the civilian "spectators" as well. They say that "a mature society . . . must eventually accept violence as an essential part of human nature, essential not because it is good or bad but essential because it is there" (p. 540). Likewise, Anthony Storr (1970), Rollo May (1972), and Henry Krystal (1982) discuss ways by which aggression can be acceptably discharged before it reaches a dangerous level, and Glover (1960) states that "crime is part of the price paid for the domestication of a naturally wild animal (man)" (p. 7). The failure to express anger and aggression are believed by analysts to result in ulcers, hypertension, and a host of other physical and social illnesses. They argue that if aggression is not regularly expressed it will build up to a dangerously high level which can then lead to excessive and spontaneous discharge. They also state that it is possible to vicariously reduce aggression by observing violence in others, a process known among social psychologists as *catharsis*.

Another aspect of current psychoanalytic theory deserves mention. According to various analytical theories it is possible for a person to invoke one or more "ego defense mechanisms" to prevent the expression of aggressive drives. (This is also said of sexual instincts where sexual energy can be denied expression and used in other, substitute endeavors, a process known as "sublimation.") Aggressive energy can be channeled into nonaggressive behavior, according to Freudian theories. Thus, it is postulated that (a) all people have aggression instincts, but (b) not everyone will behave aggressively, owing to the use of various defense mechanisms. This kind of internal ambiguity makes psychoanalytic theories difficult, some would say impossible, to test in any scientific fashion. It is largely for this reason—that almost any finding can be interpreted within the framework of the theory—that it is still considered viable by many. However, it is just such a state of omniscience that is the theory's greatest source of vulnerability. It is, in terms of philosophy of science, not falsifiable (Popper, 1959); that is, it cannot be disproven even if it is false.

With regard to those parts of the theory that are amenable to test, such as the notion that aggression regularly and inevitably increases with the passage of time, and that aggression can be discharged vicariously, almost all have failed to receive support from empirical research (Quanty, 1976). Of the testable hypotheses from psychoanalytic theory, the most controversial is the catharsis notion, which predicts that viewing or engaging in violence will discharge the observer's level of aggression. While there are some studies supporting such an idea (e.g., Bramel, Taub, & Blum, 1968; Feshbach & Singer, 1971; Fromkin, Goldstein, & Brock, 1977; Konečni, 1975), most research on the issue finds that, rather than reducing aggression, observing violence increases it (e.g., Bandura, 1965b; Berkowitz, 1970c; Malamuth & Donnerstein, 1984; Tavris, 1982). Even those studies that yield support for the psychoanalytic position can be interpreted more readily in other, nonpsychoanalytic ways (Hokanson, 1970). The catharsis issue is discussed more fully in Chapter 2.

In the Minds of (Mostly) Men

From this point forward, I will deal only with human aggression except in those instances in which animal data may serve as a useful source of hypotheses to be tested with humans. In terms of the flexibility of behavior, contemporary psychologists often speak as though human, like much animal, aggression is highly stereotypic, consisting of characteristic forms of expression. Anthropologists have known for some time that human aggression—if it is present in a society at all—can be expressed in a wide variety of ways, and that these particular forms of expression are learned. As early as 1939, Boring, Langfeld, and Weld could write:

> conflict between individuals does not invariably or universally result in the same behavior. Instead of fighting with his fists, the Kwakiutl Indian fights with property in the institution of the "potlatch," in which the more property he can give away or destroy, the more superior he is to his opponent. Eskimos settle their conflicts in a public contest in which each sings abusive songs about the other. When two Indians of Santa

Marta quarrel, instead of striking each other they strike a tree or rock with sticks, and the one first breaking his stick is considered the braver and hence the victor. In other societies aggression is expressed in still other ways; even within the same society there may be a wide range of different socially approved expressions of aggression. (p. 163)

If we look further at non-Western cultures, we find little evidence that aggression is universal. Of course, all that needs to be done to refute the hypothesis that it is a universal instinct, as the psychoanalysts or sociobiologists would have it, is to point to those societies that show no overt signs of violence. Ashley Montagu (1978) has done that.

Many human societies cannot be characterized as aggressive. . . . There are societies in which both inter- and intragroup aggression is low, as among the Toda of Southern India, and there are societies in which both inter- and intragroup aggression are nonexistent, as among the Tasaday of Mindanao, in the Philippines . . . the Punan of Borneo, the Hadza of Tanzania, the Birhor of Southern India, the Veddahs of Ceylon, the Arapesh of New Guinea, the Australian aborigines, the Yamis of Orchid Island off Taiwan, the Semai of Malaya, the Tikopia of the Western Pacific, the Land Dayaks of Sarawak, the Leppchas of Sikkim, the Papago Indians, the Hopi, the Zuni, and the Pueblo peoples generally, the Tahitians, and the Ifaluk of the Pacific. (pp. 3–5)

It must be pointed out that these cultures represent only a small portion of humanity. One might wish to argue that these few nonaggressive cultures are in some sense mutations, exceptions to the rule that we are an innately violent species. As Segall (1983) has argued, however, "The mere fact of difference across societies in degree, form, and concomitants of aggressive behavior is, in our view, an overwhelming problem for instinct theorists and sociobiologists. We doubt that they are equipped to solve it by remaining within their theoretical frameworks" (p. 4). What the existence of these peaceful peoples demonstrates is that, whether or not aggression is innate in humans, it is within their means to do away with it. As Goode (1969) has argued:

> That few men do kill or maim others seems to refute the notion of a biological urge or instinct to murder. Whatever man's aggressive impulses, obviously most men learn to control them. Much more compelling, however, are the great differences in homicide and assault rates among nations, regions within nations (e.g., the southern United States or Italy as compared with the north), classes and ethnic groups, the two sexes. The differences are so great as not to be explicable, except by reference to *social* factors. (p. 943)

Neither the evidence from animal or psychophysiological research nor from psychoanalytic and anthropological research justifies the conclusion that as a species we are all the carriers of violent impulses which are bound to find expression.

What Do The Media Tell Us About Violence?

A few years ago I was at a meeting of the International Society for Research on Aggression in Mexico City at which more than 50 papers were presented. These covered the broad range of aggression, violence, and peace research—human and animal brain studies, a model for predicting war presented by a distinguished political scientist, studies on personality and violent crime, and anthropological analyses of the control of aggression. From these many varied and interesting papers, only one was written up in the English-language press—a study of an experimental drug that inhibits mouse-killing in rats (Potegal & Glusman, 1983; Powledge, 1983). Why weren't the political, social, and psychological bases of violence also presented in the press?

I began collecting all articles on violence, aggression, and crime research appearing in three leading American newspapers (*Los Angeles Times, New York Times, Washington Post*) and three newsmagazines (*Newsweek, Time, U.S. News & World*

Report) between 1982 and 1984. The focus of the analysis was on the underlying model of human violence that might result in the selective reporting of research. While results of the study are not yet complete, I have several distinct impressions from reading scores of such articles (Goldstein, 1986b). Foremost among them is the *mechanistic* view of behavior implicit in journalistic accounts of research on violence and crime (Rosnow, 1981). Although some of the articles discuss research on social and psychological factors involved in violence, there is a consistent theme that (1) the causes of human violence exist within the individual, (2) that if only psychiatrists, psychologists, and biologists were clever enough, they could identify the genetic or personality factors that give rise to violent behavior, and (3) given the "fact" that the causes of violence reside within the individual's skin, it is assumed to be at least theoretically possible to identify potential offenders before they ever commit an offense by using some sort of early childhood screening procedure. It is also the case that a good many psychologists, psychiatrists, anthropologists, and other scientists employ these assumptions. The hard evidence for this "model" of human aggression is lacking.

What are the implications of such a perspective? One is to reinforce the belief that those who commit crimes or acts of violence are different in tangible and predictable ways from those who do not. Second, this view also undermines the offender's own sense of efficacy and social responsibility by suggesting that he is impelled to act antisocially. There is a self-fulfilling prophecy in this view of criminality. Many individuals who commit violent crimes hold the same beliefs about aggression as the rest of the population (having learned them from the same sources—the mass media). They also believe, and argue in court, that their crime was uncontrollably caused by a physical or psychological (rather than a personal or moral) defect.

Why do we so often pin our hopes for explaining violence on a biological, genetic, or physiological entity? Perhaps the primary reason for this reductionist emphasis is an attempt to separate ourselves (who act in an acceptable manner) in a tangible way from those whose behavior we deplore. We can feel comfortable, satisfied, and relatively safe knowing that we do not possess the dreaded abnormality. If we convince ourselves that the lawless and the violent are qualitatively different, we are then in a position to treat them expediently, since they are not completely "normal." If we ourselves should commit an act of violence, then our own individual responsibility for it is minimized to the extent that our behavior was impelled by tangible and uncontrollable forces.

It is tempting to adopt the reductionist position, not only because it serves to make us complacent, but because we have so often been exposed to it. In countless tales, films, books, and television programs we have seen individuals whose violence was the result of brain damage, schizophrenia, physical agents such as drugs and alcohol, and "bad genes." Social and psychological causes of violence, which are abstract and therefore more difficult to portray, are less often implicated in accounts of crime and aggression (Dorfman, 1984; Goldstein, 1981, 1986b).

Scientists, no less than others, tend to be reductionist in their belief that aggression's ultimate explanation will be biological. Because sound research methodology is difficult to achieve in the study of intangible causes of behavior, theory development suffers. Since theory on the origins of human violence is relatively weak, scientists tend to take the path of least resistance and ascribe aggression to biological necessity. The problem is thus "explained." For example, Freud initially attempted to explain the presence of human aggression in terms of the life instinct, but he was unable to account for the atrocities of war in this way. So he proposed an aggression instinct, and events became more readily "understandable." Another reason scientists tend to reject social and psychological explanations for violence is that many of these theories have been so simple and one-dimensional. If one tries to account for aggression in purely sociological terms, such as social class and status deprivation, there are counterexamples that cannot be easily fit within the theory. For example, some have argued that aggression is found most often among the poor and powerless, but they immediately encounter the fact that most people who are poor and feel powerless are not aggressive, despite the fact that most aggression may be committed by individuals fitting such a description. Clearly additional factors must be invoked to account for why only some poor and powerless people are aggressive while the majority are not. These factors have so far eluded sociologists. Of course, counterexamples do not indicate that a theory is false, only that it may be too simple. It is, in fact, desirable in science to arrive at the simplest theory permitted by the data, and scientists often resort to the simplest of all possible theories, that people behave the way they do because they are genetically programmed to do so.

A major objection to the notion of instinct is that it is not subject to empirical test; there is no ethical way to demonstrate scientifically that any complex social behavior is an instinct in humans. In recent years, even those who study animal behavior have softened their notion of what an instinct is. No longer is an instinct believed to be a purely internal impulse to engage in a specific behavior. In most circumstances external environmental requirements must be satisfied before an "instinct" is expressed. Tinbergen (1951) has suggested that the term "instinct" be replaced by the concept *fixed-action pattern* to indicate that the behavior is not spontaneously *emitted* by the organism, but is most typically *elicited* by external stimulation in conjunction with some internal state of readiness of the organism. Even here, however, the situation is far more complex than a simple interaction between the organism and the environment. "Even for nonhumans . . . the interaction of organism and environment is far from the simplistic models offered by biological determinism. And this is much more the case for our own species. All organisms bequeath to their successors when they die a slightly changed environment; humans above all are constantly and profoundly making over their environment in

"Not guilty by reason of genetic determinism, Your Honor."

Cartoon by Robert Mankoff. Reprinted with permission. Copyright © 1982 by *The New Yorker.*

such a way that each generation is presented with quite novel sets of problems to explain and choices to make; we make our own history, though in circumstances not of our own choosing" (Lewontin, Rose, & Kamin, 1984, p. 13).

It would be unwise to accept the aggression instinct hypothesis in the absence of sound evidence on its behalf. To accept it prematurely would also lead us to accept aggression, crime, and war as inevitable. This in turn would put us in either a passive position with respect to the eradication of such behaviors or in the position of eugenicists, attempting to control violence through repression or selective breeding (Kevles, 1985). This is not to deny that biology sets limits on human behavior. The infant at birth is potentially many people (though not an infinite number), and the person the infant becomes is determined by what happens to him or her, when, where, and with whom. It is safe to say that we are all born with the capacity and potential for learning to behave violently. After all, we are capable of using our hands, feet, and teeth to punch, kick, and bite. We are capable of learning to design weapons for destruction. However, to argue that we instinctually use our hands, feet, teeth, and toolmaking abilities to inflict damage on our fellow humans requires a leap of (non)faith that is not justified by scientific evidence.

Human Cognition and Aggression

The antecedents of violent crimes as reported by the offenders themselves have always impressed me as extraordinarily petty (Wolfgang, 1958). Homicides are reputedly committed because a person finds a word or gesture unacceptable or threatening. In a crowded bar, someone is jostled by a stranger; he pulls out a knife and stabs the person who pushed him. A husband and wife argue over inconsequential matters that come to have fatal consequences. Humans are the earth's supremely symbolizing creatures. We are able to impart meaning of near infinite variety to any object or action. A piece of multi-colored cloth may evoke feelings ranging from disinterest to nationalistic fervor, depending upon whether it is the flag of an unknown country or that of the Third Reich. We can find in a small gesture or subtle glance worlds of meaning, capable of eliciting feelings, thoughts, and actions far in excess of such barely noticeable stimuli.

Certainly one of the distinguishing characteristics of our species is this symbolizing capacity. It enables us to represent the most complex of ideas using only marks of ink on a page. It makes possible the planning of a trajectory for a retrievable space vehicle, but also the planning of a trajectory for a nuclear weapon. If humans as a species appear always to have been more destructive than their circumstances warrant, it is not because they have been bequeathed this excess genetic baggage from their primate ancestors. Rather, it is because the very capacities that allow us to shape our environment to suit our convenience also allow us to perceive threats and enemies where none exist. We can even imagine on the basis of barely tangible artifacts that other species are innately violent. There has never been destruction of the human type or scale in any known species. We did not obtain our aggressiveness through those genes we share with other species; it is not their fault. We obtained our capacity for violence along with our ability to reason abstractly, to see things, like gravity or threats, that are not materially there. We are the only species capable of aggressing because of the beliefs we hold. The uniquely human abilities that make Bach's B-minor Mass possible also gave rise to Auschwitz.

The Unity of Human Aggression

When confronted with a large and diverse set of elements one way to simplify and make some sense of them is to sort them into categories (usually with a large pile reserved for "miscellaneous"). Students of human aggression have often attempted to reduce the complex and varied acts of aggression in which humans have engaged by subdividing aggression into various types and then proceeding to explore one or more of these types. However, in the absence of any sufficient reason for parsing aggressive behavior, we ought to begin with the assumption that aggression is a uniform behavior; that the factors that underlie and determine one act of aggression are also those that determine other acts.

Historically, there have been three bases which have led scholars to categorize aggressive acts into subtypes—theoretical, empirical, and legal. Theoretical bases for dividing violence into various types generally stem from the fact that different theories are capable of explaining and predicting only limited instances of aggression, and so theorists have divided aggression into types depending upon their ease of explanation. Empirical bases for categorizing aggression stem from the fact that different acts of aggression have, or seem to have, either different antecedent conditions or different amounts of force, premeditation, or emotional arousal involved. Thus, distinctions are often made by social psychologists between "angry" aggression, which assumes the actor to be emotionally excited immediately prior to his aggressive act, and "nonangry" aggressive behavior (Berkowitz, 1962, 1984). The target of aggression has also been used as a basis for distinguishing types of violence. According to the frustration–aggression theory, first proposed in 1939 by Dollard, Doob, Miller, Mowrer, and Sears, aggression can be displaced onto a target other than the frustrator in an act of "displaced aggression." Attacking the initial frustrator would be an example of "direct aggression." The means and amount of activity involved in an act have been used by Buss (1971) to categorize aggression. Buss' typology is presented in Table 1.1. All of the "active" varieties of aggression clearly fit within our definition of aggression; they all involve the intentional delivery of physical or psychological injury to another. The passive

TABLE 1.1 A Typology of Human Aggressive Behaviors

	Active		Passive	
	Direct	Indirect	Direct	Indirect
Physical	Punching the victim	Practical joke; booby trap	Obstructing passage; sit-in	Refusing to perform a necessary task
Verbal	Insulting the victim	Malicious gossip	Refusing to speak	Refusing consent, vocal or written

Source: Adapted from "Aggression Pays" by A. H. Buss, 1971, in J. L. Singer (Ed.), *The Control of Aggression and Violence*, p. 8, New York: Academic Press. By permission of author and publisher.

varieties are also designed to cause psychological injury to others and, therefore, also meet our criteria for aggression. Whether or not such distinctions have any bearing on our interpretation and explanation of violence remains to be seen.

Moyer (1968, 1976) has categorized animal aggression into several types, depending upon the physiological mechanisms involved in the aggression and the conditions under which the behavior is displayed. But even these types of animal aggression are not found in all species, and there is no a priori reason to expect all of them to be present in humans. Furthermore, human behavior is considerably more modifiable by experience and learning than lower organisms', and so humans are unlikely to respond "automatically" to any internal or external set of conditions.

American and English law also make distinctions between kinds or degrees of violence. Some violence is perfectly legal, but legal violence has its bounds (Mummendey, 1984, Smith, 1983). While it is legal to physically punish a child, it is illegal to batter a child. The distinction is only one of degree, and the law is not very precise on the dividing line. Illegal acts of violence may be categorized on the basis of victim, forethought, intentionality, means, or age of the aggressor. Aggressive acts committed by juveniles are distinguished from those committed by adults; acts involving a law enforcement officer or federal agents as victims are often distinguished from those involving private citizens; acts which are premeditated are legally distinct from those which are "spontaneous"; acts committed while engaged in another crime, such as a felony, are seen as legally distinct from those not so committed; and violence which is intentional is legally different from that which is accidental. The law also allows for acts committed while the actor was in some way unable to exert cognitive, rational control over his or her own behavior, such as violence committed in the heat of passion or while "temporarily insane."

What are we to make of these various characterizations of aggression? Since our goals are to provide explanations for aggression and means to control and eliminate violence, we will have to approach this problem from the perspective of these aims. We have seen in the preceding pages that several factors may serve as contributory causes of aggressive behavior, such as electrical brain stimulation and the XYY Syndrome. It is conceivable, though it has by no means been proven, that individuals with certain genetic or organic disorders may be violence prone. Such people, whose violence is beyond their desire or control, would be excluded from the present analysis since it is questionable whether their behavior has the intention necessary to qualify as aggression. Nevertheless, even if their aggressive behavior is not designed to injure others in any conscious way, their actions are certainly destructive of others and would be considered aggressive by most observers. For the purposes of our analysis, however, we will generally exclude organic disorders since it is unlikely that those who suffer from them aggress with the conscious intention of injuring others.

Much aggressive and destructive behavior is only tangential to some other behavior. Most police officers who are killed while on duty are shot by people intent only on avoiding arrest for some other crime; their immediate intention is not the injury of a police officer, but the avoidance of arrest. Nevertheless, we would have to consider such behavior to be within the realm of our definition of aggression since there can be little doubt in the actor's mind that shooting a gun at someone is likely to injure or kill the person. Even though the aggressor's immediate intention is not the injury of the police officer, his actions while bent on escape are designed to injure and, therefore, even though his behavior is what many would call "instrumental" (that is, designed to achieve some end other than the injury of another), it is nonetheless aggressive. The distinction between an aggressor with a genetic or neurological disorder, which in some sense impels him to violence, and a felon acting to avoid apprehension, is a psychological or cognitive one. In the former case, the actor does not have the ability not to aggress, while in the latter case, greater choice is present. It is the ability to choose—to intend—which makes the felon's behavior aggressive.

A General Model of Aggression

In order to provide some structure and continuity to the discussions that follow, a simple model of aggressive behavior is presented here to serve as a guide in examining various instances of human aggression. Aggressive behavior is a complex act, based on a number of simultaneously acting factors. In order for aggression to occur, there must be some impetus to aggress, inhibitions against aggressing must be overcome, and the situation—in terms of the opportunity and ability to aggress and the availability of a target—must be appropriate. Given these aspects of every act of violence, any model of aggressive behavior will have to incorporate these factors within it.

It is proposed here that two sets of opposing tendencies operate in any potentially aggressive situation: tendencies to aggress and tendencies not to aggress. (See also Megargee, 1972.) The aggression expressed is a product of this conflict. The decision of whether or not to aggress in any particular situation depends upon the relative strength of these two opposing tendencies. When the number and strength of all the pro-aggression factors outweigh the number and strength of the anti-aggression factors, aggression will ensue. When the anti-aggression factors are stronger than the pro-aggression forces, no aggression will result.

We can divide the pro- and anti-aggression factors into long-term factors and situational factors. *Long-term* factors are those which are relatively enduring, or personality characteristics of the individual, such as his or her norms, attitudes, and values toward aggression, prior experiences with aggression, and knowledge of and ability to use aggressive or nonaggressive strategies in interpersonal disputes. Likewise, in any given instance, there are situational idiosyncrasies which may facilitate or inhibit aggressive behavior. These immediate, *situational* factors often play a prominent role in any act of violence. Although subsequent chapters are devoted to these four components—long-term and situational factors associated with tendencies to aggress and with tendencies not to aggress—a brief discussion of each will be given for the sake of clarity.

Long-Term Factors Facilitating Aggression

The primary source of enduring factors toward aggression is the socialization of the child. During socialization, the child acquires a set of values, norms, attitudes, beliefs, and expectations about aggressive behavior. These long-term norms[1] are usually acquired through selective reinforcements from, and the examples set by, one's parents, peers, and teachers. Although no two individuals are apt to share identical norms about the appropriateness, means, or desirability for aggression, large groups, such as whole societies or subcultures within any society, are likely to have many norms in common (Campbell, 1984; Sutherland & Cressy, 1966; Wolfgang & Ferracuti, 1967). For example, most Americans learn that aggression is desirable when used in defense of country, self, personal property, or the law.

These long-term norms, once acquired by an individual, are relatively stable and are likely to remain unchanged during one's lifetime. Two reasons can be given for the persistence of such norms. First, the individual is likely to have continued contact with others who share his or her norms and with those from whom he or she acquired them initially. A considerable body of evidence indicates that people are most likely to be attracted to others who share their basic attitudes, values, and norms (Byrne, 1971). Second, once norms are acquired, one's subsequent experiences and beliefs are organized around and integrated within one's existing normative framework. Basic norms and values, then, become the bulwark of subsequent beliefs and experiences (Rokeach, 1973).

Norms are acquired through processes of experience, modeling, and conditioning, and the agents of such learning include

1. The term *norm* is used here as a shorthand notation signifying values, beliefs, attitudes, and expectations.

parents, peers, and teachers, as well as informal social agents, such as symbolic figures of authority as depicted in books, newspapers, movies, and television. In the next chapter we will examine such learning processes.

Situational Factors Facilitating Aggression

Given that an individual may have positive norms toward aggression, it is still the case that even the most violent individual is not perpetually violent, and even the most passive among us is likely to be instigated to aggression under certain circumstances. The circumstances which facilitate aggression are considered under the heading of situational factors. Among such factors are those which diminish normal inhibitions against aggressing, such as familiar environments, the presence of friends and relatives, victims associated in the actor's mind with aggression, and alcohol. Other situational factors discussed in Chapter 3 are the presence and availability of a weapon, emotional arousal and frustration, and physical environments which facilitate anonymity of the actor and his actions. Any factor which momentarily raises one's tendencies to aggress or lowers one's restraints against aggressing will be considered a situational pro-aggression factor.

Long-Term Factors Facilitating Nonaggression

At the same time that people learn which situations, targets, and means are appropriate for aggression, they also learn which situations, targets, and means are inappropriate. In our society we tend to learn that certain people are inappropriate targets of violence, such as the sick, the aged, and young children. We learn which specific behaviors are admissible in a fight and which behaviors are taboo; which situations are "aggressible" and which are not. *Aggressible situations* would include barrooms, public streets, vacant lots; *nonaggressible locations* include other peoples' homes, theaters, churches. Although these informal rules are sometimes broken, people in general are less likely to aggress in nonaggressible than in aggressible situations and are less likely to attack victims who are not deemed to be acceptable targets for aggression rather than those who are. Given these informal and generally recognized rules, we would have to conclude that an actor who aggresses against an old woman in a church would be acting more aggressively (in the sense that he has violated more taboos to overcome more resistance) than one who engaged in precisely the same physical acts against a 30-year-old man in a barroom.

One reason for treating pro- and anti-aggression systems independently is to stress that there may be factors that encourage nonaggressive behavior which are not simply the absence of factors that encourage aggression. In other words, people may learn positive forms of social behavior rather than mere inactivity as an alternative to violence (Staub, 1971). One person may deal with interpersonal conflict by being nonaggressive because of the fear of the consequences for acting aggressively, while another may act nonaggressively because of the belief that disputes ought to be resolved by verbal arbitration. Thus, not acting aggressively does not mean precisely the same thing as acting nonaggressively.

Situational Factors Facilitating Nonaggression

Even the most violent people tend to be nonviolent in most circumstances. The situational factors that are likely to reduce aggression are the presence of a potentially punishing agent, such as a parent or police officer, an unfamiliar environment, unfamiliar potential victims, easy identifiability of the actor and his actions, a strong sense of individuality or self, and the presence of nonaggressive others. These and related factors are discussed in Chapter 4.

How do these four sets of factors combine to determine aggression? Since aggression is viewed as the result of a conflict, the probability of aggressive behavior is given by the ratio of pro-aggression elements, both situational and long-term, to anti-aggressive elements, situational as well as long-term. (See page 108.)

Each of the factors in the model can be perceived as more or less important by different people or by the same person at different times. Thus, it is implied by the model that aggression conflict is based not only on the simple sum of pro- and anti-aggression factors but also on their relative importance to the individual involved. According to the model, one reason that aggression occurs is because a variety of norms and values may be in conflict with one another. It should be noted that this is quite a different notion than the one proposed by a number of sociologists (most notably Emile Durkheim) who view aggression and antisocial behavior to be the result of too few norms, a state referred to as *anomie*.

The model is essentially a conflict model, and several immediate consequences of this fact should be indicated. First, the behavior (aggressive or nonaggressive) engaged in by an individual in an interpersonal situation is the result of a number of factors. Second, the relationship of any single element to aggression will depend upon the number and type of other elements present, both as part of the individual's personality as well as the immediate situation. Third, in viewing aggression as the result of a cognitive or mental conflict, we would expect the act of aggression to have cognitive consequences. As we shall see in Chapter 3, aggressive behavior (and nonaggressive behavior as well) has reliable cognitive effects, among which are reevaluation of the social situation, of the victim, and of the conflict. Fourth, since the number of pro- and anti-aggression elements in any given situation may vary from individual to individual or from time to time, there can be different quantities of conflict present immediately prior to the decision to act (or not act) aggressively. The effects of differing amounts of conflict may be seen in the length of time it takes the actor to decide which behavior to engage in and in the intensity of the act. The more conflict present in any given situation, the longer it will take to decide whether to act aggressively or not. Although very few studies have measured the time it takes to respond aggressively (Goldstein, 1985a), it is expected to be longer in high-conflict situations than in low. This may be due to the need to consider more elements and to resolve the conflict more fully prior to behaving overtly. In addition, when conflict is high, there will be more postbehavior cognitive consequences of the act. When there are both many and strong reasons to act aggressively combined with many and potent reasons for not acting aggressively, conflict is high and the mental work required to resolve the conflict in the actor's mind is considerable. Once the decision has been made to act aggressively, the intensity of the act will be stronger than if conflict were less. This is because of the need to justify one's actions, and there is less justification for violence in high than in low-conflict situations (Brock & Buss, 1962). Thus, high-conflict situations lead us to the following hypotheses: (a) the more conflict present, the longer it takes for the individual to act; (b) the more conflict present, the more intense the aggression; (c) the more conflict, the more cognitive consequences of the aggression, such as in reevaluation of the situation, the action, or the victim. These ideas are explored more fully in Chapters 3 and 4.

We turn now to a detailed examination of each of the four components of the model plus an examination of related phenomena which complement the model.

2

Development and Maintenance of Aggression

Aggression and violence vary in three ways: by culture, by individual, and by circumstance. Cultural differences in human aggression, such as those discussed in Chapter 1, are so dramatic as to preclude a purely biological explanation of violence. Instead, one must explain the ways in which human cultures vary and how those cultural differences are related to variations in aggression. However, within each culture there are also two sources of variance in aggression that need explanation. First, some individuals are clearly far more, and some far less, aggressive than the typical person in that culture. How are we to explain these differences between individuals? Second, any given individual is more aggressive at certain times and in certain circumstances than in others. How best to explain these intraindividual differences?

In this chapter we focus on those factors that influence an individual's chronic level of aggressiveness. Among the processes discussed are the learning of aggression and aggression-related norms and attitudes from parents, peers, and other "models." We also explore those impersonal models, both real and fictitious, portrayed in the mass media that teach aggression, some-times inadvertently.

Let us first examine one of the basic assumptions of much aggression research, that within any culture individual levels of violence vary considerably from one person to another. Like so many behaviors and psychological traits, it is probable that aggression and related attributes are normally distributed in the population of any given culture. The norm or average level of aggression does vary from one person to another, but a per-tinent question concerns the variance of aggression: How much more violent is one member of a culture than any other? Upon inspection, the differences between people's aggressive-ness appear to be relatively slight, more apparent than ac-tual, hovering around the cultural mode. For instance, in the United States, most parents physically punish their children on occasion, and the difference between simple discipline and child abuse is found to be more a matter of degree than of qualitative type of behavior. Frequently the difference between a case of simple assault and one of homicide is the ready availability of a lethal weapon (Morris & Hawkins, 1970). Of course there are obvious, and often highly publicized, cases of individuals with long histories of violence. We know from cohort studies that a small number of juveniles commit a disproportionate amount of crime (Farrington, 1983; Wolfgang, Figlio, & Sellin, 1972). What is less widely known is the degree to which crimes are committed by seemingly "normal" individuals. Often these "normal" crimes are influenced by conditions in the individual's immediate environment.

To summarize, the following points are offered: (a) each person engages in acts that are more or less violent, depending on the individual's culture; (b) within each culture, there is a typical or modal amount of aggression, though individuals within that culture vary considerably from one to another; and (c) each person has a characteristic or chronic level of aggressive-ness, with variations depending upon the immediate circum-stances. Over a long period of time, an individual may be more or less aggressive than others. In statistical terms, we may speak of this as an individual's *modal level of aggression*.[1] Differences between people in the modal level of aggression will be discussed in the present chapter, while variation in the aggression level of a given individual at different times will be discussed in Chapter 3.

Learning Aggression

As Feshbach (1970) has stated: "All theoretical models of aggression assume that aggressive behavior is, to some degree, acquired. The disagreements among theorists lie in the importance ascribed to learning as a determinant of aggression and in the kinds of aggressive behavior that are assumed to be influenced by past learning" (p. 173). In this section, we examine the means by which aggressive behavior and related norms and attitudes are learned.

A distinction is made by learning theorists between classical and operant learning or conditioning. In *classical conditioning,* some neutral object is paired with an object that normally causes a particular response. After repeated pairings, the neutral object is then capable of leading to this same response. This type of learning was first described in the classic studies of Pavlov (1927). In Pavlov's experiments, dogs, which normally salivate when presented with food, came to salivate at the sound of a bell after it had been presented several times in conjunction with the food.

A second kind of learning, most often associated with B. F. Skinner but which can be traced to the psychologist E. L. Thorndike, is called *operant conditioning.* In this type of learning, rewards presented to an actor after a response is made

1. The mode is one kind of statistical average. It refers to the most frequent or typical item in a series. The modal level of aggression is the typical level of aggression shown by an individual in a wide variety of situations and under a wide variety of circumstances.

serve to strengthen that response and increase the likelihood that it will occur again, while punishments presented after a response decrease the probability that the response will be repeated. Naturally, there are variations on and complexities to these procedures, but these two types of learning form the basis for most of the behavior patterns that relatively simple creatures, like animals and infants, acquire. Further, it has been shown that aggressive behavior patterns learned by young children are likely to persist into adulthood, particularly so for males (Kagan & Moss, 1962; McCord, 1983; Olweus, 1979).

Aggressive behavior—and more importantly, norms, values, beliefs, and attitudes about aggression—can be learned from one's parents and later from teachers and peers through classical and operant processes and imitation. If aggression is spoken of in favorable terms by one's parents, for example, then the concept will come to have positive value for the child (Loew, 1967). If a child is encouraged to be or is rewarded for being aggressive, then the child is likely to increase his or her use of aggressive behavior in future encounters with others (Geen & Pigg, 1970).

In most situations, though, children are not provided with indiscriminate rewards for acting aggressively nor is aggression spoken of in the home in uniformly favorable terms. Rather, parents, teachers, and peers may reward or speak approvingly of aggression directed toward particular targets, such as Jews or blacks, but offer no such rewards or approval for aggression directed toward other individuals or groups. There are two consequences of such discriminations. First, the child may perceive the behaviors of others as inconsistent with regard to when aggression is appropriate, or those who do reward the child may, in fact, be inconsistent in their actions. Such inconsistency, particularly from parents, is frequently seen as one cause of aggressive behavior among children (Yarrow, Campbell, & Burton, 1968). Second, the distinctions between targets made by others, while they may to some extent be adopted by the child, are likely to be rather fragile and tenuous, that is, the

fine distinctions which adults may make with regard to targets
of aggression the child may be cognitively unable to make or
maintain. Therefore, "acceptable" aggression directed toward,
say, Jews, may generalize to other targets, such as members of
other religious minorities. However, the learned targets of aggression defined as acceptable will more often serve as victims
than other targets to which the learning generalizes (Berkowitz,
1984).

In the same way that children learn which groups or individuals are considered appropriate targets of aggression by their
parents and peers, they also learn to value (or devalue) weapons and other means of aggressing, the circumstances under
which aggression is considered appropriate, and attitudes toward the police and the law (Berkowitz, 1970b, Berkowitz &
LePage, 1967; Caprara, Renzi, Amolini, & Dimperio, 1984).

A well-known study by Sears, Maccoby, and Levin (1957)
examined child-rearing practices and children's aggressive behavior. Nearly 400 mothers of kindergarten children were interviewed about their use of disciplinary measures, their permissiveness toward their children's aggressive, feeding, and sexual
behavior, and their children's expression of aggression toward
peers, siblings, and parents. Among the major findings of the
study was that the use of physical punishment by parents was
positively related to the amount of aggression shown by the
children. When coupled with high permissiveness toward the
children's behavior, high punishment was even more strongly
associated with children's aggression. Over one-third of the
girls and two-fifths of the boys rated as highly aggressive came
from homes in which parents relied on physical punishments as
a disciplinary measure and also were highly permissive.

Although the methodology of this study may have some short-
comings (Yarrow et al., 1968), it raises questions about the use
of physical punishment in child-rearing. According to traditional learning theory, if children are punished for being aggressive, they should then refrain from aggressing in the future.
Yet the results of research on punishment, particularly physical

punishment, and children's aggression often show that punishment only begets aggression. What, if anything, do children learn when they are punished for some transgression? Countless parents have discovered, much to their chagrin, that their children do as they do and not as they say they should do. The theory that speaks most directly to child-rearing, aggression, and crime is Albert Bandura's social-learning theory.

A "Trickle-Down" Theory of Crime: Social-Learning Theory

Putting more money into the pockets of the wealthy is believed by conservative economists ultimately to benefit the middle and lower class. This is often referred to as the "trickle-down" theory. Its validity in the field of economics is questionable; however, there are areas where people clearly are influenced by those above them in economic or social standing. Fashion, for example, generally moves from the top to the bottom of the social hierarchy. The dress of the leisure class tends to become the dress of the middle class. One reason for the popularity of television soap operas is that they enable middle-class people to see how the wealthy (presumably) dress and behave. Tastes in food and recreation move from the top to the bottom of the social structure. The values of the upper class also tend to be adopted by others. In this sense, partly because of their visibility and partly because they embody our notion of success, the wealthy wield a disproportionate influence on the demeanor, values, and actions of the population as a whole. This is not to say that behavior at the top is not also influenced by the behavior of those lower in the social structure. Certain fashions, particularly of the young, are apt to be emulated by older people who are typically higher in the social structure. Generally, though, people focus their attention upwards in the pecking order.

It is one argument of this chapter that crime flows downward in the social structure. As Supreme Court Justice Louis Brandeis wrote, "Our government is the potent, the omnipotent teacher. For good or for ill, it teaches the whole people by its example." The kind of crime that individuals at different positions in the social structure are capable of, or have opportunities for, committing are different. Politicians, judges, and other public officials are in positions to take bribes and receive kickbacks from contractors. White-collar workers are in a better position to evade paying taxes or to embezzle funds than blue-collar workers or the unemployed. Those at the bottom of the social system are more likely to commit crimes where they confront their victims, such as armed robbery and burglary.

This view of crime and society is based largely on social-learning theory and an impressive amount of research in support of it (Bandura, 1965b, 1973, 1977). According to Bandura, children learn not only from direct rewards and punishments, but also from observation. It would take children considerably longer to learn to speak if they had to rely solely on rewards and punishments for correct and incorrect verbal utterances; instead, they are able to imitate the verbal speech patterns of those around them. The ability to imitate is seen as one mechanism by which learning occurs. As Bandura states,

> it is difficult to imagine a socialization process in which the language, mores, vocational activities, familial customs, and the educational, religious, and political practices of a culture are taught to each new member by selective reinforcement of fortuitous behaviors, without benefit of models who exemplify the cultural patterns in their own behavior. (p. 5)

Models, that is, others whose behavior serves as a guide to observers, are capable of teaching both concrete actions as well as abstract concepts to a child. Obviously, the most important models are a child's parents, from whom the child acquires a wide variety of behavior patterns, attitudes, values, and norms. According to substantial research (Bandura, Ross, & Ross, 1967; Steuer, Applefield, & Smith, 1971) a child will learn behavior which it observes in others, providing that neither the others nor the child-observer are punished for that behavior.

In the case of a parent spanking a child for behaving aggressively, a conflict is presented to the child. On the one hand, the child is "told" via the punishment that aggression is intolerable. On the other hand, the child observes the parent acting aggressively. In such a case, the child is likely to learn not to suppress his or her aggression but to use it to influence the behavior of others. Naturally, if children are punished each time they are caught behaving aggressively, they are likely to learn not to be aggressive in the presence of their parents. They will also learn that, if their parents use aggression in punishing them, then at least in some circumstances aggression must be a desirable and appropriate behavior. It is not surprising, then, that aggressive parents have aggressive offspring (McCord, 1983; McCord, McCord, & Zola, 1959; Tanay, 1969).

Parents are not the only models in a child's life. If they were, children would be duplicates of their parents, and as their tastes in music and fashion demonstrate, they are hardly that. What other forces influence the child's social and moral development? One is the behavioral and moral code as embodied in the actions and pronouncements of others in the society at large. These general social norms are portrayed in the behavior of those real and fictitious individuals with whom the child has contact not only in face-to-face encounters, but in stories, books, and the mass media. (See Table 2.1.)

Aside from direct reinforcement from and modeling by parents, there are several ways in which social behavior is transmitted to the child. One of them is the behavior of adults displayed on television and in films. Children in the United States spend an average of more than 5 hours per day viewing television (Comstock, Chaffee, Katzman, McCombs, & Roberts, 1978; LoSciuto, 1972; Lyle & Hoffman, 1972). By age 16 the average American child has spent more time before a television set than in a classroom. He or she has witnessed more than 18,000 homicides and countless assaults, rapes, and abductions (Smith, 1985). Advertisers spend hundreds of millions of dollars annually in the belief that television has an effect on view-

TABLE 2.1   Criminal Models?

COAST MAYOR SUED OVER CAMPAIGN FINANCES.   "The California Fair Political Practices Commission filed a $1.2 million suit today against Mayor Roger Hedgecock of San Diego and five political associates." (*New York Times*, 16 October 1984)

FORMER OFFICIAL GUILTY IN BOSTON.   "Federal jury says ex-mayor's aide illegally covered up currency transactions." (*New York Times*, 27 June 1984)

HOUSE REPRIMANDS IDAHO REPUBLICAN IN FINANCIAL DISCLOSURE CASE.   "The House of Representatives voted overwhelmingly today to reprimand Representative George Hansen, an Idaho Republican, for failing to comply with Federal law that requires public officials to disclose their financial holdings." (*New York Times*, 1 August 1984)

PISANI, A FORMER STATE SENATOR, IS GIVEN 4-YEAR PRISON TERM IN FRAUD CASE.   (*New York Times*, 2 August 1984)

EX-NEW ENGLAND OFFICIAL INDICTED ON COUNT OF ATTEMPTED EXTORTION.   "A Federal grand jury today indicted a former Somerville Mayor who had been regional administrator of the Federal General Services Administration on a count of attempted extortion." (*New York Times*, 15 August 1984)

MICHIGAN MAYOR GUILTY OF EXTORTION CHARGE.   "Mayor Donald Bishop of suburban Dearborn Heights was convicted today by a Federal jury of trying to extort up to $250,000 from several companies seeking the city's cable television franchise." (*New York Times*, 1 September 1984)

GOVERNOR OF LOUISIANA IS INDICTED BY JURY INVESTIGATING STATE GRAFT.   (*New York Times*, 1 March 1985)

CHICAGO JUDGE INDICTED IN CORRUPTION INQUIRY.   "Cook County Circuit Judge Richard F. LeFevour, his cousin and six other people were indicted today as part of Operation Greylord, the undercover Federal investigation of judicial corruption here. . . . Judge LeFevour was indicted on 72 counts of racketeering, mail fraud and tax evasion over fourteen years." (*New York Times*, 15 November 1984)

ROCHESTER FANS BARRED AFTER VIOLENCE AT GAMES.   "It is not that basketball games are unpopular in Rochester. They are perhaps too popular, say school officials, who last Monday instituted a ban on spectators because of outbreaks of violence in the stands." (*New York Times*, 17 December 1984) ers' attitudes and behavior, and it is reasonable to examine the effects of such a pervasive medium on the social development of its most ardent viewers, the young. Second, children can learn behavioral and normative patterns from the games and sports that society condones. At home and in school children participate in play activities that adults believe will teach them general rules of conduct which they are then able to use in other, nonplay, situations. Other forms of entertainment may also provide the child with rules of conduct. The behavior of people whom the child learns about secondhand also provides the child with expectations and norms that guide his or her actions. Each of these forms of social learning is reviewed below.

Might Makes Right: Teaching Violence in the Media

Imagine that scores of times each day images of violence against Jews were telecast into millions of American homes. People would be outraged and would demand that such incitement to anti-Semitism be halted. It is not Jews, but another group, that is singled out as the victims of televised and filmed violence—women. In one television melodrama after another young women are kidnapped, assaulted, raped, and murdered. What effects do such incessant portrayals of violence have on their audience?

More research has been conducted on the effects of violence in the mass media than on almost any other topic in the realm of human aggression. After nearly three decades of research social scientists are now almost unanimous in their agreement that portrayed violence increases aggressive behavior. The research, with some notable exceptions (e.g., Feshbach & Singer, 1971; Hennigan et al., 1982; Milgram & Shotland, 1973), is highly consistent and warrants some firm conclusions about the effects of televised and filmed on violence on human aggression (Freedman, 1984).

The National Institute of Mental Health (1982), in a summary of research on television and behavior, concluded that

the consensus among most of the research community is that
violence on television does lead to aggressive behavior by children and teenagers who watch the programs. This conclusion
is based on laboratory experiments and on field studies. Not
all children become aggressive, of course, but the correlations
between violence and aggression are positive. In magnitude,
television violence is as strongly correlated with aggressive behavior as any other behavioral variable that has been measured. The research question has moved from asking whether
or not there is an effect to seeking explanations for the effect.
(p. 6)

In order to provide the reader with a deeper appreciation of
research in the area of media violence, one of the most influential studies that has had a major impact on subsequent research
and theory will be reviewed in detail (Bandura, 1965a).

Bandura exposed 66 nursery-school children to one of three
5-minute films on a TV console. In all three films an adult enacted a series of verbal and physical attacks on a plastic Bobo
doll (a large inflatable doll with a painted face and a weighted
base). One group of children observed the model rewarded
with candy and soft drinks following the aggression. A second
group of children saw the model punished following the aggression with spanking and verbal rebukes. A third group of children saw only the model's aggressive behavior with no rewarding or punishing consequences. The children were then allowed
to play for 10 minutes in a room which contained, among other
toys, (surprise!) a Bobo doll. During the play period, the children's aggressive behaviors were observed and recorded. Following the free-play period, children were told that they would
receive fruit juices and picture booklets if they would imitate
the behavior that they had seen in the film. The children's aggression during the free-play period is an index of the extent to
which the films influenced "spontaneous" aggression, while their
behavior during the last phase of the study represents the extent to which they learned and could reproduce the aggressive
behavior they had seen in the films. Spontaneous aggression was

greatest in the groups which had seen the model rewarded and which had seen the aggression without any reinforcing consequences; it was least in the group which had seen the model punished for aggression. Thus, punishment may serve to inhibit spontaneous aggression among children-observers. When asked to imitate the aggression they had seen, all three groups of children were equally able to duplicate the model's aggressive performance. Thus, learning of aggression took place regardless of whether the model was rewarded, punished, or neither.

The implications of this study are many and varied. They indicate that children are capable of learning what they see, regardless of the presence of rewards or punishments. Second, the results suggest that children are likely to imitate the aggressive behavior they observe in mass media providing that the aggressor was not punished for his or her actions. Finally, the results indicate that, contrary to many theories of learning, new forms of behavior can be acquired in the absence of rewards.

A considerable number of studies have been conducted along the lines of the Bandura experiment, most of which were designed to determine whether observers, either children or adults, could (or would) imitate the aggressive behavior depicted in mass media. With only occasional exceptions (see Freedman, 1984) such studies have demonstrated that media violence is capable of producing real-life violence.

The evidence for a reduction or catharsis of aggression following observation of violence is far outweighed by the scores of studies reporting that the observation of violence serves to stimulate aggression. It is conceivable, however, that a kind of catharsis does occur under some, as yet unspecified, conditions. In order for a genuine aggression catharsis to occur, there should be a reduction in aggressiveness but not in other, unrelated responses. For this reason, research on aggression should measure at least one nonaggressive response in order to determine whether the effects observed are specific to aggressive behavior or not.

In addition, many of the laboratory experiments on imitation of media violence have been criticized on methodological grounds, largely because the research laboratory is an artificial environment and because most laboratory experiments use excerpts of violent scenes taken out of context from the film or TV program. Finally, nearly every study on effects of media violence has been conducted using only Americans as research subjects, and there is the question of the generality and pervasiveness of the results.

Together with my colleagues Ralph Rosnow and Tamas Raday of Temple University, Irwin Silverman of York University, Toronto, and George Gaskell of the London School of Economics, I (1975) conducted a media-aggression study in four countries (Canada, England, Italy, and the United States), using a natural, nonlaboratory research setting, with full-length films. We chose films playing in each country which were aggressive (such as *Clockwork Orange* and *Straw Dogs*), or which were equally arousing, but nonaggressive (such as *The Decameron*), or which were neither arousing nor aggressive (such as *Fiddler on the Roof* and *Living Free*). We interviewed adult males either before or after they had seen one of these films. The interview was designed to assess the viewer's level of punitiveness, which was used as an index of aggressiveness. For example, we asked our subjects to assign minimum prison sentences for persons convicted of various crimes, and more severe prison sentences were taken to imply more punitiveness on the part of subjects. There was a statistically significant increase in this aggressiveness measure after viewing an aggressive film in all four countries, while there was a general decrease in aggressiveness after viewing a nonarousing, nonaggressive film. Sexual films had no appreciable effects on observers' levels of punitiveness (see Figure 2.1). The study as a whole indicates that (a) aggressive films have an effect on viewers' levels of aggression; (b) the results are not peculiar to Americans, but also hold for Canadian, English, and Italian viewers; (c) the increase in aggressiveness was due to the aggressive content of the film rather than to its arousing qualities, since arousing but

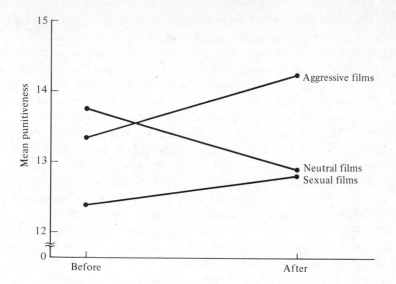

Figure 2.1 Effects of film content on aggression. (Data adapted from Goldstein, Rosnow, Raday, Silverman, and Gaskell, 1975. By permission of Mouton Publishers, The Hague, Paris.)

nonaggressive (that is, sexual) films did not influence observers' aggressiveness levels. As an additional part of the study, some of the nearly 900 subjects in this study were asked to donate money to charity either before or after watching one of the films. There were no significant changes in charitableness as a result of any of the films. This is evidence that the aggressive films may have an influence only on subjects' levels of aggressiveness, rather than have a general effect on all behaviors.

The research having demonstrated that media violence can influence aggressive predispositions, a number of additional questions become prominent. For example, does media violence influence some people more than others? Why is there so much violence on television and in movies and in books? What other behaviors and attitudes are influenced by modeling and imitation?

Television viewing does not occur in a vacuum but rather takes place within a family context. The importance, meaning, and psychological experience of watching television will depend upon the quality of one's home environment, just as so many other behaviors are influenced by family interactions.

Largely because of learning unrelated to TV viewing, males seem to respond to TV violence to a greater degree than females. In the Bandura study summarized earlier, both spontaneous and learned aggression were found to be greatest for boys. This is probably because boys are provided with greater opportunities and rewards for aggression than girls, and because boys are more apt to identify with adult males and thus have more numerous aggressive models to emulate than girls. The quality of parental training also influences the effects of televised violence. Chaffee and McLeod (1971) report that in families where nonaggression is stressed (for example, where parents teach their children not to be mean to others), there is only a slight relationship between viewing media violence and aggressive behavior in children (although the relationship is still a positive one). In families where there is no stress placed on nonaggression, there is a strong relationship between viewing TV violence and aggressive behavior. Another way of stating this is that in homes where parents serve as strong nonaggressive models for their children, televised models will be relatively uninfluential; where parents fail to serve as nonaggressive models or where parents encourage aggression, televised models will either take precedence over parental models or will serve to further strengthen the child's aggression. If mass media models contradict parental models, it is likely that the parental models will be more influential, since it is the parents who directly control the child's rewards and punishments. It has often been suggested that the influence of mass media violence is greatest for young children who are unable to distinguish reality from fantasy. The research on this question, however, fails to support this contention. Even while recognizing that violence on television is fictional and staged, adults too have been found to become more aggressive following exposure to media violence (Berkowitz, 1965; Wolfe & Baron, 1971).

It has also been argued that whatever influence televised violence has, it is short-lived. Again, the research indicates that, to the contrary, the effects of exposure to media violence may persist for months (Kniveton, 1973) or years (Eron, Huesmann, Lefkowitz, & Walder, 1972).

Attraction to Violence, or
What's Playing at Your Neighborhood Theater?

If media violence is so likely to have detrimental effects on social behavior, why is it so prevalent and why do people expose themselves to it with such regularity? It is a curious phenomenon that people who, for the most part, consider themselves peaceable feed on violence so often and in so many forms. As the Hearst newspapers discovered long ago, spectacular and violent headlines sell papers, and as the entertainment industries discovered more recently, violence in movies, television programming, comic books, and novels attract a sizeable audience. Clark and Blankenburg (1972) found a strong and positive relationship between the percentage of TV programs classified as violent in any given year and the average Nielsen ratings for that year. In addition to the fictional portrayal of violence, people are attracted to more direct forms of aggression. Children play with toy weapons, adults rush to the scene of a conflagration and gather in large numbers to watch a threatened suicide or the aftermath of a violent crime. Nearly 17 million people attended professional football games in 1983 and probably four times that number watched them on television. Boxing matches, particularly those involving heavyweights, are broadcast by satellite to millions of people, and soccer is the world's number-one spectator sport. It is undeniable that a good many people find violence appealing rather than appalling.

Several years ago, the Philadelphia newspapers carried an advertisement for a forthcoming movie, *The Mark of the Devil*, which was described as "Positively the most horrifying film ever

made. The first film rated V for violence." The ad is reproduced
in Figure 2.2. As I happened to be in the neighborhood when
the film opened, I was curious to see who would attend *The
Mark of the Devil*. I was surprised to see a very long line before
the box office. Most of those in line were boys in their early
teens, and nearly all of them were black.

Why should young blacks, who, like other city-dwellers, are
undoubtedly exposed to considerable violence in their schools
and neighborhoods, pay to see a film advertised as extraordinarily violent? If we assume, as many do, that there is an innate
aggressive drive that must find expression, then violent events
may serve as safety valves which indirectly discharge aggressive
impulses in ways which are not socially disruptive. We have
seen in Chapter 1 that such an explanation is not valid; the evidence largely disputes the notion of an aggression instinct. Another explanation for the attraction to violence is based on increased familiarity with real violence in daily life (Cline, Croft,
& Courrier, 1973). Perhaps art imitates life, in the same way
that research on mass media violence suggests that life imitates
art. It seemed reasonable that familiarity with violence simply
has the effect of making violence salient, meaningful, and attractive. A third possible reason for the appeal of media violence is that it provides excitement and arousal which may be
missing from one's daily routine. Furthermore, perhaps witnessing fictional violence can help a person cope with the real violence to which he is exposed; one might learn from the film's
characters that violence can be overcome, that it is not really to
be feared.

There exists only one study on attraction to violence. Following the murder of a coed on the University of Wisconsin cam-
pus, three social psychologists conducted a study on movie preference (Boyanowski, Newtson, & Walster, 1974). There were
two films playing locally during the week of the murder, one a
violent film (*In Cold Blood*) and one based on a D. H. Lawrence story (*The Fox*). The researchers report an increase in
attendance of 63 percent among coeds at the violent film fol-

Figure 2.2 Advertisement for *Mark of the Devil* (Reprinted by permission of Hallmark Pictures, Boston, Massachusetts.)

lowing the murder, but no such increase (+13 percent) at the nonviolent film. They explain these results by suggesting that the film would help the young women to cope with their fear by exposing them to violence that would be harmless to them personally. As the authors themselves mention, however, there are a number of other possible explanations for these results, and so I decided to conduct another study which examined preference for aggressive films (Goldstein, 1972).

In this study, college students read one of three prose passages—aggressive, sexual, or neutral (that is, neither aggressive nor sexual). They were then asked to indicate which movies from a list of three aggressive, three sexual, and three neutral movies they would most like to see. The results indicated that subjects who read the aggressive passage preferred aggressive movies to all others. Those subjects who read the sexual passage showed the greatest desire to see sexual films, and those who read the neutral passage least preferred to see sexual and aggressive films. It would seem that prior experience with aggression is positively related to a preference for aggressive movie content.

There thus seems to be a continuous interplay between media violence and real violence, with an exposure to either one contributing in some measure to the other. For at least some people, exposure to media violence contributes to aggressive behavior; and for people exposed to some episodes of real violence, there is an increased preference for violent portrayals in the mass media. This diet of violence is not unlike our diet of sugar. Exposed early in life to added sugar in baby foods and cereals, the child comes to crave sugar, despite its unwanted effects.

The Role of Modeling and Imitation in Impulsivity and Self-Control of Aggression

One important abstract behavior style related to aggression is impulsiveness. "Even the simplest, most primitive steps in socialization require learning to defer one's impulses and to express them only under special conditions of time and place, as seen in toilet training. Similarly, enormously complex chains of deferred gratification are required for people to achieve the delayed rewards provided by our culture's social system and institutions" (Mischel, 1971, p. 380).

The inability to delay gratification—impulsivity—is both directly and indirectly related to aggression and criminality (Barndt & Johnson, 1955; Brock & del Guidice, 1963; Graham, Doubleday, & Guarino, 1984; Kipnis, 1968; Marohn, Offer, & Ostrov, 1971). As Mischel notes, many rewards provided by society require the ability to postpone immediate but small rewards for long-term but larger rewards. For example, high-paying jobs require planning, extended education, training, and apprenticeship. The inability to make such long-range plans and immediate sacrifices would all but preclude an individual's attainment of high occupational status. Those who lack the ability to plan for the future may be deprived of the means by which to obtain desirable social goals. Thus deprived of socially acceptable means, highly impulsive people may "improvise" their own means to such desirable goals as money, status, and power. This analysis is similar to and complements one proposed by Robert K. Merton (1957). Merton discusses, under the heading of "innovation," those in society who desire socially defined goals, such as wealth, but who lack socially approved means of attaining those goals. In this situation, individuals will provide innovative means for achieving goals which may be socially deviant or criminal.

In addition to instituting their own socially deviant means to social goals, highly impulsive people are also likely to react with aggression to interpersonal difficulties. Violence is a tempting and impulsive solution to interpersonal problems. It is tempting because it has the effect of reducing the complexities and subtleties normally found in human problems to a simple contest of strength and agility. In reducing complex interpersonal confrontations to simple physical contests, their multifaceted nature need not be considered. Reason and restraint in the face of difficulties indicate that one recognizes more than one side to a problem and that compromise might be a reasonable way to settle the dispute. Communication and compromise between disputants is often a tedious, long, and complex process, particularly so if the parties begin from different vantage points. Differences of opinion, if not of fact, make one's arguments likely to distortion and misinterpretation by those who hold divergent views.

How can delay of gratification be learned? An important experiment by Bandura and Mischel (1965) demonstrates that it can be acquired through processes of imitation and modeling. Children with little tendency to delay gratification were exposed to a model who, when given a choice between an immediate small reward and a future larger reward, chose the latter. Children who tended to delay gratification were exposed to a model who chose the immediate small reward. Both groups of children, when tested following exposure to the respective models, showed significant changes. Low delay of gratification observers became better able to delay immediate gratification, while children initially high in delay of gratification tended to become lower. These results suggest that the kinds of postponement and planning for rewards demonstrated by parents and others to whom the child is exposed will influence the child's own such tendencies.

As with the effects of aggressive models, the family's social environment mediates the child's responses to delay of gratification in models. In particular, the child's expectations of and trust in others influences his impulsivity. To the extent that the child has trust in others, there is a tendency to imitate modeled delay of gratification; when trust in others is absent, the child will tend to be impulsive and low in the ability to postpone immediate rewards (Mischel & Staub, 1965; Stumphauzer, 1972).

Impulsive behavior implies that conscious, cognitive mechanisms which normally influence behavior are absent. What psychologists refer to as cognitive control over behavior, and what we generally call self-control, is minimized when a person acts impulsively. Rather than taking the time to decide among several possible alternatives and rather than trying to imagine the consequences of one's actions for oneself and others, impulsive behavior reduces a person's rationality and choice.

Aggression in Sports

Games and sports serve a variety of functions—from teaching young participants to abide by formally proscribed rules of conduct to the fostering of competition between teams and cooperation within teams. Both participants and spectators may learn abstract principles for behavior from the rules of games. With respect to those sports where bodily contact between participants of opposing teams is inevitable, it is possible that for some (or even all) players and for some (but certainly not all) spectators, the aggression inherent in contact sports is peripheral to other facets of the game. It is reasonable that for some players and perhaps for some spectators, the violence of, say, a football game, can be transcended through involvement in the game and in this way have little effect on the spectators' or players' levels of aggression (Goldstein, 1982a). For a great many spectators and players, however, aggression in contact sports does have an effect.

There have been numerous occasions when violence has erupted at athletic events. Lever (1969) has suggested that the war between El Salvador and Honduras may be traced to a soccer match between those countries. In 1964, a riot erupted at a soccer match in Lima, Peru, in which 300 people were killed. In 1974, thousands of fans burned down the soccer stadium in Honduras after two matches had been suspended. Soccer fans have been killed and officials beaten at riots in Sicily (June 1983), New York (May 1983), Colombia (November 1982), and Bangladesh (June 1984). And in May 1985, 37 soccer fans were killed at an England-Italy match played in Brussels. In addition to the score of boxers' deaths in recent years, boxing fans have engaged in violence at bouts in New York and Philadelphia. Hockey players and fans have rioted with monotonous regularity. High school, college, and professional football fans have created increasing security problems for management (*New York Times,* 13 March 1984). Similar examples of outbursts of violence are not difficult to find at any body contact sport (Mann, 1979). On the other hand, despite the recent emergence of "punk tennis" and the growing violence of baseball and basketball, sports crowds tend to be better behaved at those sports that do not revolve around body contact. Indeed, there is apt to be a close correspondence between the amount of violence on the playing field and the amount of violence in the stands (Russell, 1983; Smith, 1979).

There are several issues surrounding violence in sports. While there appears to be an increase in the amount of sports-related violence, we do not really know whether this is so. In the not too distant past, brutality in sports was merely accepted without comment. Today it is apt to lead to litigation. What once was considered part of a sport is now viewed as behavior that occurs within a larger social framework. When sports were seen as strictly local affairs—before the advent of widespread television broadcasting of sports—violent behavior was likely to be thought of as inherent to the game. Once teams lost their local quality they began to be seen by sports fans as business franchises, and thus the social norms and laws that govern business and other forms of social intercourse increasingly were applied to behavior in sports. The fact is that we do not know whether the incidence, prevalence, or severity of sports violence is increasing, decreasing, or remaining constant. In a domain where statistics of every imaginable sort are kept with fervor, no official record of violence in sports is maintained.

Nevertheless, we may examine the impact and the causes, if not the magnitude, of sports violence. We can consider whether the physical contact of boxing, football, hockey, and soccer is in any way responsible for violent outbursts among fans. We may also consider a larger issue, the extent to which aggressive sports provide social support for aggression in general. Thus, we can inquire into both the immediate, short-term effects as well as the general, long-term effects of aggression in sports.

As we have seen in the studies on mass media violence, observers tend to learn and imitate the violence they witness on the movie and television screens, and it would be reasonable to expect that watching violence in sports, like watching it on TV, tends to increase the likelihood of observers' becoming aggressive. Further, we have seen that the effects of televised violence are not necessarily immediate, but may develop later and persist for quite some time. There is no sound reason for expecting the effects of violence in sports to differ from the effects of violence in other forms of entertainment.

However, a number of students of human behavior have suggested, to the contrary, that participation in and observation of aggressive sports serve as safety valves that tend to reduce participants' and observers' levels of aggression. Among those who have proposed such a catharsis of aggression have been William James (1911), Freud (1930), Ardrey (1966), and Lorenz (1966). Storr (1970) has proposed that "rivalry between nations in sports can do nothing but good" (pp. 132–133). Of course, if these theories are incorrect and observing or acting out violence causes an increase, rather than a decrease, in aggressiveness, then their suggested policies of fostering international competition are not only incorrect, but potentially disastrous; while trying to reduce aggressiveness, they will actually increase it.

There are, besides these two extreme positions (the one suggesting that watching aggressive sports uniformly leads to an increase in aggression, and the other suggesting that it leads to a reduction), several intermediate theoretical positions. Based on the frustration-aggression theory of Dollard and his colleagues (1939), it would be expected that watching aggression would lead to an increase in aggression only for those observers who are in some way frustrated. At a soccer match or football game, for example, it would be frustrating if a person wanted Team A to win while Team B actually won. Thus, we might predict that only those spectators whose preferred team loses a game would show an increase in aggression, while those whose preferred team wins would show no increase, or perhaps even a decrease, in aggression.

Following the study of Bandura elaborated earlier, we might consider that watching a team lose a game in an aggressive sport is in some way perceived as a "punishment" for their behavior, while watching a team win a game is perceived as a "reward" for their behavior. If this can be applied to an aggressive sport, we might expect those who watch their preferred team win a game to become more aggressive than those who watch their preferred team lose the game since those in favor of the winning side have seen their players rewarded for their aggression, while those favoring the losing side have seen their team punished for its aggression.

In order to examine these various possibilities, Robert Arms and I (1971) conducted a study at an Army-Navy football game in which we measured male spectators' levels of hostility before and after the game. As a control, we also measured hostility among spectators before or after they had observed an Army-Temple gymnastics competition. This nonaggressive sport served as a check on the possibility that watching *any* sport for 2 or 3 hours would lead to an increase in aggressiveness. We obtained hostility scores from 150 spectators at the football game, 97 of them before the game and 53 following the game. We also obtained information about their favored team and their level of involvement in the game. At the gymnastics meet we obtained comparable kinds of information from 81 male spectators, 49 before and 32 after viewing the meet. The major findings of the study, shown in Table 2.2, indicate a significant increase in hostility for spectators at the football game and no such increase for those observing a gym meet. The increase in hostility at the football game did not depend upon whether the spectators' preferred team won or lost or on whether they even cared who won or lost; all groups of spectators interviewed after the game had a higher hostility score than those interviewed before. It will be noted that the increase for the pro-Army subjects was greater than that for the pro-Navy subjects.

TABLE 2.2   Hostility at Aggressive and Nonaggressive Sports

| | Football game Preferred team | | | |
	Army (winning team)	Navy (losing team)	No preference	Gym meet
Pre-game	10.42	11.72	11.67	12.00
Post-game	13.33	13.17	15.00	12.71

Note: The higher the score, the more hostile the subjects. Each entry is the mean hostility for subjects in that group.

Source: Adapted from "Effects of Observing Athletic Contests on Hostility" by J. H. Goldstein and R. L. Arms, 1971, *Sociometry, 34,* 83–90. Used by permission.

The largest increase in hostility, then, was for those who favored the winning team rather than the losing team. This finding lends support to the social-learning and imitation theory of Bandura. The pro-Army fans saw Army players rewarded for their aggression on the field, while pro-Navy fans saw their team punished (by being defeated) for their aggression. Thus, the vicarious reward served to heighten Army fans' aggressiveness and the vicarious punishment served to inhibit to some degree the aggressiveness of Navy fans (although the latter still showed a significant increase in hostility).

This study has since been replicated by Arms, Russell, and Sandilands (1979), who examined the effects of ice hockey and professional wrestling (using swimming as a control event) on spectators' levels of aggression. College students were randomly assigned to attend one of the three sports events, and their aggressiveness was measured with three different scales (Buss-Durkee Hostility Inventory, Nowlis Mood Adjective Check List, and a punishment index developed by Goldstein, Rosnow, Raday, Silverman, & Gaskell, 1975). Where significant changes occurred on these measures, they were in the direction of increased aggressiveness after watching both realistic (hockey) and stylized (wrestling) forms of aggression. The highly competitive but nonaggressive swim meet produced no change in the hostility of the observers.

Even the broadcasting of body contact sports seems to influence aggression. An intriguing, though controversial, study by Phillips (1983) reports that the televising of heavyweight championship boxing matches leads to a perceptible increase in the U.S. homicide rate!

The Olympic Games and Warfare

It has been demonstrated by Sipes (1973) that those cultures in which aggressive sports are prominent are also those in which warfare is most common. Of course, the very basis for the modern Olympic Games is to foster international understanding, thus reducing the likelihood of war. Baron Pierre de Coubertin, who revived the modern Olympic Games in 1896, conceived of the Olympic Games as "a great quadrennial festival of sports thereby creating international respect and goodwill and thus helping to construct a better and more peaceful world."

What is the relationship between participating in the Olympics and the construction of a more peaceful world? In a study by Keefer, Goldstein, and Kasiarz (1983), the relationship between these two events was determined for 60 countries for the period 1896 to 1965. Those countries with greatest Olympic Games participation (number of athletes sent to the Olympics, statistically corrected for each country's population size and density) were the most likely also to have engaged in a disproportionate amount of international violence (measured in number of months spent at war). Some of the data on the relationship between participating in body-contact sports in the Olympics and war are shown in Table 2.3. Of those 30 countries that entered more than the modal number of body-contact sports, 18 of them were involved in two or more wars. Of the 30 countries below the median in number of body-contact sports entered, only 6 participated in two or more wars.

This study does not mean that there is a causal connection

TABLE 2.3 Warfare and Participation in Body-Contact Sports of the Olympic Games

Frequency of War	Number of Body-Contact Sports Entered	
	Below Median	Above Median
Below median	24	12
Above median	6	18

$\chi^2 = 8.40$, $df = 1$, $p < .01$.

Source: Adapted from "Olympic Games Participation and Warfare" by R. Keefer, J. H. Goldstein, and D. Kasiarz, 1983, in J. H. Goldstein (Ed.), *Sports Violence*, p. 189. New York: Springer-Verlag. By permission of authors and publisher.

between sports and warfare. Most likely, both participating in aggressive sports and waging wars reflect a nation's values and ethos. Countries with little interest in combat are unlikely to display an interest in combative sports.

The recent Olympic boycotts clearly suggest that we may endow athletic events with highly affective and symbolic meaning. If we insist on viewing international athletic events as contests of national or ideological superiority, they will continue to have effects on political behavior.

If a nation's attitudes toward violence attenuate the relationship between Olympic Games participation and warfare, perhaps the individual sports fan's attitude toward aggression is also important in determining the effects of witnessing violence. Research has indeed demonstrated the role of such attitudes. In an experiment by Berkowitz and Alioto (1973), the same aggressive football and boxing scenes were preceded by either a neutral introduction or by one stressing hatred between the opponents. In the latter case, observers were significantly more aggressive toward someone who later angered them. (Zillmann, Bryant, and Sapolsky, 1979, suggest that the spectators would have found the latter events more enjoyable, as well.)

An interesting field study was conducted at a professional ice-hockey game by Harrell (1981). Hockey fans were asked if fighting should be allowed to go unpenalized "because it is an important part of the game." Those active hockey fans who answered "yes" to this question (about half of them) were more hostile after the first and second periods of the game than fans who were intolerant of aggression. Thus, the fan's tolerant attitude toward sports violence mediates the effects of witnessing the violence. It is tempting to conclude that one's own attitudes not only help to determine the effects of witnessing sports violence, but that observing sports violence also strengthens the individual's attitudes.

"Russia Outlawed Forever. Bombing Begins in 5 Minutes." The Case of Hostile Humor

Jokes do not often make the news, but in the summer of 1984, President Ronald Reagan, in testing the microphone for a radio broadcast, joked about outlawing and bombing Russia. The remark created an international furor (*New York Times,* 14 August 1984). The London *Standard* headlined "President's Nuclear Joke Misfires." *Le Monde* called it a gaffe and invited the comments of psychologists to decide whether the joke was an expression of repressed desire. The Polish press agency called it "irresponsible behavior" that could alienate voters "by the easy talk of a man who has shown he would do anything to fuel up the arms race." The Dutch news service expressed the hope that the President tests his missiles more carefully than he tests his microphones.

To what extent is the telling of or laughing at hostile jokes related to other aspects of aggression? Does the President's joke tell us anything about his "repressed desires" or his behavioral intentions? At least two questions about aggression and humor seem pertinent to our interests. First, does telling or laughing at an aggressive joke make the teller or recipient more (or less) aggressive? Second, what psychological meaning can be attributed to telling or laughing at aggressive humor? That is, is a person who laughs vociferously at, or who continually tells, aggressive jokes more aggressive than those who rarely tell or laugh at such humor?

The initial interest in studies of aggressive humor was the popular notion that it serves as one of the "safety valves" for aggression; that by telling or laughing at aggressive humor a person could somehow "let off steam," thus making actual aggressive behavior less likely. This effect, known as catharsis of aggression through humor, has been proposed by Freud (1905), Grotjahn (1957), and other psychoanalysts. Their underlying argument is that some of the energy that might otherwise be expressed in overt aggression is siphoned off during laughter and thereby serves as a drain on aggressive energy. The net result is theorized to be an overall reduction in potential aggression.

Experiments on the humor-catharsis effect have provided no support for its occurrence. In one study, Berkowitz (1970a) reports that college students who heard an aggressive Don Rickles tape became more aggressive than those who heard a nonaggressive George Carlin tape. Comparable results have been reported by others using various kinds of humor, including animated cartoons (Ellis & Sekyra, 1972; Mussen & Rutherford, 1961; Zillmann, 1983). These studies demonstrate that rather than serving as a drain, aggressive humor actually stimulates aggressive behavior. Indeed, it would be surprising if exposure to aggressive humor had different effects than exposure to aggressive sports, television programs, or parents. There is no reason to expect aggressive humor to differ from other types of aggressive stimuli.

We have heard a great deal lately about the positive effects of humor. Norman Cousins (1971) attributes his recovery from a serious illness in part to the use of humor, and the belief is widespread that humor of any sort is beneficial (Goldstein, 1982b). What research has made clear in the last few years is that the aggressive content of some humor (or films or television programs) may have effects independent of the context or the medium in which it is embedded. Just as it is the violence often contained in sexually explicit films, and not the sexual content, that influences observers' aggressive behavior (Malamuth & Donnerstein, 1984), so it is with aggressive humor. On the other hand, nonaggressive humor (or nonviolent erotica) may arouse responses, such as positive emotions, that are incompatible with aggressive behavior. In these cases, exposure to (nonaggressive) humor may lower the probability of aggressive behavior (Baron, 1983; Baron & Ball, 1974).

Telling a joke is a means of communicating not only a humorous incident to someone else but also of presenting oneself in a particular light (Fine, 1983; Oring, 1984). It is a statement about oneself encapsulated in a witty remark. President Reagan's joke about bombing Russia was certainly compatible with his negative attitudes toward the Soviet Union. But his joke may have reflected less his intention or unconscious desire than his self-presentation as a hard-liner vis-à-vis the Soviets.

When is aggressive humor used? Generally, aggressive jokes are directed toward those individuals or groups of higher social position or greater power. Gunnar Myrdal (1944) noted that much humor among American blacks in the 1930s and 1940s was directed at whites, and Obrdlik (1942) found that many jokes circulating among the Czechs during the German occupation were directed against their Nazi oppressors. Theodor Reik (1962) argues that the use of aggressive humor by Jews was an effective weapon against their oppressors and was, in many instances, the only avenue of attack open to them. There is probably good reason for the use of this fairly subtle and indirect form of aggression—because of humor's ambiguity, it is less likely than direct attack to result in retaliation. Aggression through humor is indirect; if disguised sufficiently it may not even be perceived as hostile by the recipient. And if the recipient should smile or laugh, even though he or she is the butt of the joke, retaliation is all but precluded.

Why Is Aggressive Humor Funny?

It is probably safe to say that most "one-liners" told by monologists and stand-up comics are aggressive in content. Henny

Youngman's one-liner, "Take my wife. Please!" is obviously aggressive in content, if not in intent. Joan Rivers and Don Rickles have built their entire repertoire around the insult, embarrassment, and antagonism of others. Aggressive humor seems to be more popular today than in the past (but it is difficult to substantiate this claim). Yet not everyone finds aggressive humor to their liking. While many are laughing at Don Rickles, others are not.

The first rule of thumb for a comic is to make his humor topical, to tap the interests of the audience. A comedian would not tell jokes about air pollution to Fiji Islanders simply because they would not have the necessary background and experiences to process such jokes. He would have to tell a joke that his audience could understand. Understanding, however, is not enough to make a joke funny. The joke would have to be one to which the audience could relate, one that would be involving and interesting to them. Our hypothetical comedian would be well-advised to tell medical jokes at a medical convention, political jokes at a legal meeting, and aggressive jokes to an audience familiar with, or concerned about, violence. In short, people most appreciate jokes whose content is familiar or salient to them (Goldstein, 1976). This conclusion is quite different from the explanation of the enjoyment of aggressive humor proposed by Freud and others. Freud proposed that people laugh at or tell aggressive (and sexual) jokes in order to relieve the tension and anxiety that these drives cause. He suggested that people appreciate aggressive jokes because society prohibits, and punishes, the free and indiscriminate expression of overt aggression. In order to prevent our aggression from building, we laugh at aggressive humor to keep our internal levels of aggression at some moderate, "safe" level.

In many experimental tests of this Freudian hypothesis, research subjects are exposed to aggressive or sexual stimuli designed to increase their internal levels of aggressive and sexual tension. Subjects then rate how funny they find aggressive, sexual, and "neutral" (nonsexual, nonaggressive) jokes. The Freudian hypothesis predicts that those who are aggressively aroused will prefer aggressive humor while those who are sexually aroused will prefer sexual humor. Most of the experimental tests support this prediction (Dworkin & Efran, 1967; Kuhlman, 1985; McCauley, Woods, Coolidge, & Kulick, 1983; Nevo & Nevo, 1983).

There is in a sense a paradox resulting from this support: Are we to infer from the psychoanalytic hypothesis that those who find bowling jokes or medical jokes amusing have some internal drive or anxiety connected with these topics? That hardly seems reasonable, and to account for the appreciation of nonsexual, nonaggressive humor, Freud proposed a quite different explanation. A question that arises from this rather complicated state of affairs is whether it is necessary to account for aggressive and sexual humor appreciation in different terms from those used to explain appreciation of other types of humor. Ideally, a single set of explanatory principles would be used to account for all humor enjoyment. So, rather than starting from Freud in our quest to understand aggressive and other humor content, we may be better off starting from scratch.

Having dispensed for the moment with the psychoanalytic theory of humor, we can return to our initial problem: Why do some people appreciate aggressive humor? As I have hinted earlier, the familiarity or salience of a particular issue might be the key to its appreciation in humor. Just as the salience of violence makes violent film content preferred to other content, so salience of aggression or sex serves to heighten the enjoyment of aggressive or sexual humor. In fact, whatever issues are salient to a person may lead to increased enjoyment of jokes revolving around those issues.

To test this hypothesis, Jerry Suls, Susan Anthony, and I (1972) embarked on a series of studies designed to determine the extent to which the notion of salience could account for enjoyment of specific types of humor content. We followed, as closely as possible, the procedure that had been used to test the Freudian hypothesis. In one experiment, we exposed our research subjects, college students, to photographs that depicted either scenes of violence and aggression or scenes of automobiles. Subjects then rated the funniness of cartoons that were either aggressive in nature or which centered on automobiles. According to predictions from psychoanalytic theory, only those subjects who had some internal aggressive drive, that is, the subjects exposed to aggressive photographs, would show a particular preference; they would seek to reduce their aggressive feelings by rating aggressive cartoons as most funny. The psychoanalytic theory would not be able to make any prediction concerning subjects exposed to automobile photographs; clearly, they should not experience any heightened tension or anxiety as a result of exposure to pictures of cars. On the other hand, the salience hypothesis predicts that whatever content area is most salient or familiar to a person will lead him to appreciate humor that centers on that particular topic. Thus, subjects exposed to aggressive pictures should most appreciate aggressive humor, while those first exposed to automobile pictures should most appreciate humor dealing with cars. The results of our studies clearly indicate support for the salience predictions. In several additional experiments designed to test the salience notion, including a cross-cultural test of the hypothesis in Africa and Japan, support was obtained in all cases. We were able to enhance the appreciation of medical and musical jokes merely by exposing subjects to stimuli of a medical or musical nature beforehand (Kuhlman, 1985).

In summary, appreciation for particular types of humor content is due largely to the salience or familiarity of that content to the humor recipient. We would expect that people to whom aggression is most familiar, say, residents of the inner city, as compared to those from the suburbs, would find aggressive humor most funny. As television has made realistic and almost instantaneous aggressive incidents available to all of us, it follows that aggression and violence become more salient to us, and this increase in the prominence of violence would heighten our appreciation for aggressive humor. This does not mean that, because we may find aggressive humor funnier than in the past, we are ourselves more aggressive. Indeed, it may reflect our increased concern with violence rather than any increased propensity to engage in it.

Models in the Public Eye

Most of the topics discussed so far have focused on the learning of aggression and related norms in children. While behavior patterns of the child are likely to persist through adulthood, learning is a continual process and adults, too, are susceptible to the influence of rewards and punishments and of models in their social environment.

There are models in adults' environments that are for the most part absent from children's. In particular, people who have already achieved prominence by virtue of their status or power are likely to serve as models for adults who aspire to such status or power.

Of singular importance to aggressive and criminal behavior would be models who have achieved some measure of success via illegitimate or aggressive means. For example, if a politician is exposed as having taken illegal contributions or kickbacks, as in the examples in Table 2.1, then those who aspire to be in a similar financial or social position become more likely to engage in illegal acts in order to achieve their goals. Successful criminals thus serve as reinforced models to observers. In addition, to the extent that such criminal models go unpunished, their illegal behavior becomes legitimized. If these arguments are correct, there should be an increase in criminality following disclosure of wrongdoing among political or public officials to the extent that the latter are seen as rewarded (for example, as successful) or to the extent that they go unpunished (Phillips & Hensley, 1984).

If the violent acts of real and fictional individuals can compel imitation, perhaps official violence, like war, can also influence the behavior of individuals. "Wars, after all, carry the full

TABLE 2.4 Homicide Rate Changes in Combatant and Noncombatant Nations

	Homicide Rate Changes		
	Decrease	Unchanged	Increase
Combatant nations	6	8	15
Noncombatant nations	9	2	3

Note: Figures refer to the number of countries in each category.

Source: Adapted from *Violence and Crime in Cross-national Perspective*, p. 85, by Dane Archer and Rosemary Gartner, 1984, New Haven: Yale University Press.

authority and prestige of the state, and wars also reward killing in the sense that some war 'heroes' are decorated and lionized, often in direct proportion to the number of homicides they have committed" (Archer & Gartner, 1984b, p. 66). Following a continual decline in the crime rate since the 1930s, the murder and non-negligent manslaughter rate in the United States more than doubled during the Vietnam War (Gurr, 1981).

Archer and Gartner (1984b) tested the notion that war stimulates domestic violence. They examined homicide rates before and after World War I and World War II for both combatant and noncombatant nations. The results, summarized in Table 2.4, reveal that the homicide rate increased for combatant nations and tended to decrease for countries that did not participate in war. War seems to legitimize and thus stimulate domestic violence.

There are also more subtle cues legitimizing illegal acts. For example, in many American cities, cars prominently display stickers or tags indicating support for the police. One reason—albeit an implicit one—for such display is as a sign to the police to deal leniently with the driver of the car in cases of illegal parking and other traffic offenses. On one level, the tags imply—whether correctly or not—that the law is flexible, that it applies, or should apply, more fully to some people than to others.

Is There a Violence-Prone Personality?

Late in 1984, Bernhard Goetz shot four young men while riding a New York City subway. He said the youths had tried to "rip him off," that he was acting in self-defense. This incident triggered (so to speak) an enormous outpouring of debate on the rights of citizens to be protected from young thugs, most of it highly supportive of Goetz's actions (Schanberg, 1985). Many people could readily understand and sympathize with Goetz's violent outburst. No one asked what kind of person would shoot four teenagers at close range. His personality did not seem to be an issue in the discussion of his behavior.

When a less explicable or sympathetic crime occurs, however, the issue of personality seems to be central. For instance, when John Hinckley attempted to assassinate President Reagan, his mental state and personal history were widely discussed and explored. People want to know "Who are these madmen capable of committing such heinous crimes?"

As these examples demonstrate, we tend to invoke the aggressor's personality as a causal explanation of violent behavior when we find that behavior difficult to understand or socially unacceptable. Was John Hinckley's behavior attributable to some basic, enduring character flaw, and Goetz's behavior to a momentary, immediate threat? This question concerns the relative contribution to violence of personality and of situations. It is one contention of this book that we have overemphasized the role of personality in aggressive and criminal behavior and ignored the powerful role played by features of the actor's immediate situation. It is more likely that violence causes personality disturbances than that personality disturbances cause violence (Carmen, Rieker, & Mills, 1985).

There are two sources of data on the relationship between personality and violence: one is based on laboratory studies of aggressive behavior and the second on studies of delinquent and criminal populations.

Personality and Aggression in the Laboratory

Laboratory experiments generally use college students as their research subjects. They do not consistently examine personality variables, but in those few studies exploring personality and aggression there are some reliable findings (Baron, 1977). Those who are anxious about or fearful of punishment tend to be less aggressive than those low in anxiety (Dengerink, 1971). Individuals who are characterized as "Type A" personalities—time-bound, driven, tense, achievement-oriented people—tend to be more aggressive than "Type B's" when they are provoked (Carver & Glass, 1977, in Baron, 1977).

When personality traits are examined in relation to situational determinants of aggression they tend to dwindle in importance. In a study by Larsen, Coleman, Forbes, and Johnson (1972), five personality traits (3 measures of hostility, Machiavellianism, and aggressivity) and five settings were explored. None of the personality traits was consistently related to aggressive behavior, but differences in the situation exerted a powerful influence on aggression. For example, subjects were much less aggressive toward female than toward male victims. After observing an aggressive model, they were more aggressive than when no model was observed. They delivered stronger electric shocks to the victim when urged to do so by others than when alone in the laboratory. Larsen and his colleagues conclude that "the situational structure is the all-important variable in predicting behavior, and that persons in fact often act opposite to their predisposition to act when faced with situational pressure" (p. 294).

One of the difficulties with laboratory studies of aggression is that subjects do not usually choose whether to aggress, but are required to aggress as part of their participation in the research. Their only choice is how aggressive to be (or they may withdraw from the experiment, which rarely happens). In actual instances of aggression the element of choice is greater.

Perhaps personality traits play a central role in violent crime, whereas they do not play much of one in laboratory studies.

Personality and the Violent Criminal

There are numerous studies of the personalities of juvenile delinquents and violent adults. So many, in fact, that it is tempting to conclude that researchers hope, despite data to the contrary, to find evidence of a "criminal type" (Rennie, 1978). Reviews of this substantial literature almost always conclude that no such evidence has materialized. When criminal types are found in one study, frequently they fail to be found in others (e.g., McGurk, 1978).

Many people assume that serious crimes, particularly those involving violence, are committed by individuals who are seriously mentally ill. This stereotype of the mentally ill is fostered by the mass media. One might read in any daily newspaper of a crime committed by "a former mental patient." The implication is clear that there is some direct connection between the crime and the individual's status as a former patient. One does not read, for instance, of a former mental patient who won an art show or saved a drowning child, situations in which the journalist assumes that there is no meaningful connection between these behaviors and having been in a psychiatric facility. Likewise, there are countless films and television dramas in which violence is committed by individuals portrayed as psychotic.

Guzé (1976) reviewed the literature on psychiatric disorders among offenders and concluded that "psychosis, schizophrenia, primary affective disorders, and the various neurotic disorders are seen in only a minority of identified criminals. There is no complete agreement as to whether any of these conditions is more common among criminals than the general population, but it is clear that these disorders carry only a *slightly* increased risk of criminality if any at all" (pp. 35–36).

In his own study of nearly 300 felons in Missouri, Guzé

found that "sociopathy, alcoholism, and drug dependence are the psychiatric disorders characteristically associated with serious crime. Schizophrenia, primary affective disorders, anxiety neurosis, obsessional neurosis, phobic neurosis, and brain syndromes are not. Sexual deviations, defined as illegal *per se,* are not, in the absence of accompanying sociopathy, alcoholism, and drug dependence, associated with other serious crime."

Of course, those characteristics associated with crime in the Guzé study are precisely those that are less easily definable and less generally agreed to be illnesses at all (Diamond, 1974, cited in Monahan, 1983).

Studies that compare inmates with the noninmate population find that there is a disproportionate number of mentally ill individuals in prison. This does not necessarily mean that they are more criminal, but may reflect the fact that a mentally ill person is more likely to be charged or convicted of a crime than someone else. This has been borne out in research by Teplin (1984), who found that "for similar offenses, mentally disordered citizens had a significantly greater chance of being arrested than non-mentally disordered persons." (It should be noted that a recent study by Steadman and Felson [1984] failed to find differential arrest rates in incidents involving ex-patients or ex-offenders.)

The MMPI (Minnesota Multiphasic Personality Inventory) has been used more than any other test to study and predict violence. Various subscales from the MMPI have been combined to arrive at different indices of dangerousness and violence-proneness. Studies on the predictive or discriminant validity of these measures have frequently yielded negative results (e.g., Holland, Beckett, & Levi, 1981; Louscher, Hosford, & Moss, 1983; Moss, Johnson, & Hosford, 1984). There are studies in which the MMPI has been used to discriminate between violent and nonviolent inmates (e.g., McGurk, 1978; Megargee, Cook, & Mendelsohn, 1967), but the ability of the test to predict future behavior remains unknown.

Overcontrolled or Undersocialized?

Megargee (1966; Megargee et al., 1967) has proposed that individuals who commit acts of extreme violence may be characterized as "overcontrolled," that is, as generally unable to express anger or hostility. Provocation builds upon provocation until some "breaking point" is reached, propelling the person into a fit of violence. There is certainly anecdotal evidence to support this view.

Many people who have committed multiple murders or attempted political assassinations have been found to be friendless introverts, drifting aimlessly from one town or job to another. Such was the case with Arthur Bremer, Sirhan Sirhan, John Hinckley, and other assassins and would-be assassins. When psychiatrists and others attempt to explain the behavior of such individuals, they tend to look within them, at their intrapsychic functioning and early childhood experiences. Rarely do they look at the individual as a social being, who derives his beliefs and behavioral tendencies from his contact with others. If there is a pattern that emerges from the information gathered on such individuals, it is that they are socially isolated. They are not close to members of their families and have few ties to any social community. John Hinckley's contacts over a period of weeks prior to his assassination attempt were confined to formal encounters with hotel personnel, waiters, bus drivers, and others with whom one engages only in formal and limited forms of interaction. These casual acquaintances described him as quiet and polite, offering no hint of the bizarre fantasies he harbored.

Perhaps the pattern of social isolation that so often accompanies depictions of violent Americans offers the key to that violence. What, after all, are the functions of social contact? One of them is to learn something about ourselves and the world we inhabit. Much of what we "know" about ourselves we know because other people tell us so. Others validate our beliefs. Social comparison theory (Festinger, 1954) presumes that individuals have a basic drive to evaluate the relative validity and credibility of their own beliefs and opinions. Since there is no direct way to do this, we turn to the only available source for self-evaluation—other people. Hence, one function of social interaction is feedback on the "correctness" of our beliefs and opinions.

In the absence of social interaction, one has little way of knowing whether a given opinion or belief is reasonable, acceptable, widely held, or idiosyncratic. The thoughts of social isolates appear to resemble autistic or schizophrenic thought— they ramble, intermix fantasy and reality, often failing to distinguish between them, flow from one topic to another in disjointed fashion, and may contain elements of violence, sex, or other highly affective content (Caughey, 1984). The reason most of us are able to distinguish realistic, "reasonable" thoughts from other, often socially irresponsible thoughts is that we have a sense of the thoughts and actions of others, of family, friends, and neighbors, derived from our contact with them or because we have read enough to have a sense of what other people believe and how they behave. No one would receive much support for the belief that a movie actress's love could be won by assassinating the President. Were such fantasies shared with others they would surely be rejected as unacceptable and unrealistic. (This does not mean that there are only a few individuals who fantasize about, and write letters to, actresses and other public figures. In America, such fantasies are so widespread as to be considered normative. See Caughey, 1984.) While little research on the behavioral effects of social isolation exists, there is evidence that it is related to social deviancy (Singer, Blane, & Kasschau, 1964).

Of course, not all bizarre acts are committed by isolated individuals. Many are committed by groups or their representatives, such as political terrorist organizations. Here it is isolated individuals who band together to form what might be called an "isolated group," one that shares a socially deviant set of beliefs and isolates its members from assessing the social validity or acceptability of its credo. This group isolation may take the form of physical segregation of members from nonmembers, swearing members to secrecy, and providing a variety of social services, such as newspapers, camps, and retail stores, to minimize social comparison with those in the mainstream of society.

This argument has several implications for the identification, treatment, and rehabilitation of violent offenders. Primary among them is the necessity to integrate offenders into the mainstream of society, where they will be exposed to socially acceptable beliefs and where they will receive negative feedback about deviant beliefs, opinions, and actions. Rather than being unable or unwilling to express their anger, many violent individuals seem to act on fantasies that stem from a lack of contact with the larger social community, or from exclusive and prolonged contact with a group that itself adheres to deviant social norms.

When personality traits are examined alongside more transient characteristics of violent offenders, such as their attitudes toward aggression, and along with situational influences on behavior, the personality traits turn out to be least predictive of behavior (Hanson, Henggeler, Haefele, & Rodick, 1984). Intelligence itself is a better predictor of delinquent behavior than most other personal traits (Hirschi & Hindelang, 1977).

For men who have committed sex crimes, such as child molestation and rape, sexual arousal in response to scenes depicting similar events is predictive of future crimes. Abel, Barlow, Blanchard, and Guild (1977) have developed an index based on sexual arousal to portrayals of rape relative to sexual arousal in response to portrayals of consenting sex. Such an index can successfully predict recidivism among men discharged from a psychiatric institution (Quinsey, Chaplin, & Carrigan, 1980). Arousal to nonsexual aggression may also predict subsequent violent behavior (Malamuth, Check, & Briere, in press).

Still, the best predictor of an individual's future behavior is apt to be his or her past behavior. Age at first arrest and number of contacts with the police are better predictors of future violence than personality traits. However, if one wishes to base sentencing or parole decisions only on these predictors, there will be too many instances of misprediction. While much crime is committed by a few individuals, many individuals who have committed a crime are unlikely to become repeat offenders. In the Wolfgang, Figlio, and Sellin (1972) study of all Philadelphia males born in 1958, over 80 percent of them had no or one arrest. Sixty-two percent of those with two arrests went on to a third, and 71 percent of those with three arrests went on to a fourth. In this chapter we have examined a number of factors associated with an individual's chronic level of aggression. A succinct summary is provided by the psychiatrist, Fredric Wertham (1969), who wrote: "Violence is as contagious as the measles." We should add that there is unlikely to be a vaccine that does not depend on the patient's will to overcome the malady. In the following chapter we examine some of those situational factors, such as aspects of the environment and transitory states of the individual, that influence criminal and aggressive behavior.

3
Situational Factors in Aggression

The chance of an American citizen's being a victim of violent crime is greater than that of being hurt in a traffic accident. The risk of being a victim is higher than the risk of being affected by divorce, death from cancer, or injury or death from a fire (U.S. Department of Justice, 1983). In this chapter we examine the role that situational factors play in violence.

Situational factors, like those associated with the learning and support of aggression, may vary in three ways:

1. Culturally, as in the availability of weapons or exposure to unpunished aggressive models, which vary widely from one nation to another.
2. Individually, as in the differential use of alcohol and drugs and emotional arousal.
3. Environmentally, being exposed to features of the physical and natural environment that encourage or restrain aggressive and criminal acts.

The situational approach to aggression and crime assumes that among people who have learned at least some aggressive behaviors, personality and early childhood experiences play only a minor role in causing violence. Of primary importance are factors present in the situation immediately preceding an act of aggression (Brantingham & Brantingham, 1981; Brier & Piliavin, 1965; Endler & Hunt, 1968; Jeffrey, 1971; Milgram, 1974). If a situation is considered inappropriate, if weapons and targets are unavailable, no aggression will occur. To stress situational and environmental variables is to ask whether anyone, given "appropriate" circumstances, might not behave criminally or aggressively.

In order to demonstrate the role of situational factors in violence, a brief summary of statistical findings on criminal homicide is presented below. This survey includes information about the nature of homicide in terms of time and place, victim-offender relationships, motives, and means.

The Case of Criminal Homicide

In his pioneering study of homicide, the criminologist Marvin Wolfgang (1958) presented a detailed examination of the 588 criminal homicides that occurred in Philadelphia between the years 1948 and 1952.

Motives

In those cases where the offender's motives could be determined, the most frequent motive precipitating homicide consisted of relatively trivial insults, curses, threats, and jostlings. These trivial motives accounted for 37 percent of all ascertainable motives. Likewise, in Great Britain the number of homicides committed for relatively inconsequential, personal motives far exceeds those committed for criminal motives and homicides committed by person considered "abnormal" (Watson, 1973). (See Table 3.1.)

Victim-Offender Relationships and Environmental Factors

Fully one-half of the 588 homicides analyzed by Wolfgang occurred between a victim and an offender who were friends or

TABLE 3.1   Murder Circumstances and Motives, 1983

Total	18,673
Percent	100.0%
Felony total	17.5
Robbery	10.6
Narcotics	2.0
Sex offenses	1.6
Arson	.8
Other felony	3.1
Suspected felony	3.2
Argument total	43.6
Romantic triangle	2.6
Influence of alcohol and/or narcotics	4.1
Property or money	2.8
Other arguments	34.1
Other motives or circumstances	14.2
Unknown motives	20.9

Note: Because of rounding, percentages do not add to 100. Murders committed during arguments while under the influence of narcotics are not counted in felony murders.

Source: Federal Bureau of Investigation, *Uniform Crime Reports,* 1983.

relatives. One hundred of the homicides involved the slaying of the offender's spouse. In only about 13 percent of the cases were the victim and offender unacquainted with one another prior to the crime, and this may be an overestimate. (See Table 3.2 for more recent figures.)

If homicides are examined in terms of their relative brutality (brutal homicides are defined by Wolfgang as those involving two or more gunshots or stabbings, or beatings resulting in death), a number of intriguing results are obtained. Whites were slightly, but not significantly, more violent than blacks in the commission of homicides. Forty-six percent of the men and 63 percent of the women victims were killed violently. Homi-

TABLE 3.2   Percentage of Homicides Reported to UCR, by
Victim's Relationship to Offender, 1982

Husband	3.4%	
Wife	4.8	
Mother/Father	1.3	
Daughter	1.0	
Son	1.7	
Brother	1.1	
Sister	0.2	
Other family	3.3	
Total family		*16.8*
Acquaintances	29.7	
Friend	3.4	
Boyfriend	1.4	
Girlfriend	1.9	
Neighbor	1.6	
Stranger	16.9	
Unknown relationship	28.1	

Note: Because of rounding, percentages do not add to 100.

Source: Federal Bureau of Investigation, *Uniform Crime Reports, 1982.*

cides occurring in the homes of the victims and/or offenders were significantly more likely to be violent than those that occurred outside the home. Spouse slayings were significantly more violent than those involving any other type of relationship between victim and offender.

With regard to location, for women offenders homicide was most likely to occur in the home (80 percent of the cases). In fact, a female who committed homicide was apt to have done so in the kitchen (29 percent) or bedroom (26 percent) of her own home. Male offenders committed homicide in their homes 45 percent of the time and on public streets or property 35 percent of the time. A man who did commit homicide in his home was most likely to have done so in the bedroom or living room and least likely to have done so in the kitchen or on the stairway.

In 94 percent of the homicide cases, the victim and offender were of the same race. (In the 6 percent that crossed racial boundaries, about half of the victims were black and about half were white.)

For female offenders, the weapon most often used was a knife (in 64 percent of the female cases), while for male offenders a handgun was the most commonly used weapon (in 27 percent of the male cases).

The victims of homicide tended to be older than their murderers and, in general, the young—those under 35 years of age—were overrepresented among offenders.

Alcohol and Homicide

One of the strongest associations found in the Wolfgang study (and in many since, e.g., Taylor & Leonard, 1983) was the relationship between the presence of alcohol in the victim or offender and homicide. In nearly two-thirds of the 588 cases, the victim, the offender, or both had been drinking just prior to the murder.

Time

Although there were no statistically significant differences between the months of the year, over 55 percent of the homicides were committed during the warmer months (April through September). Nearly two-thirds of the homicides occurred on Friday, Saturday, and Sunday, and half the homicides occurred between the hours of 8 P.M. and 2 A.M. (These are also the days and times during which most alcohol is consumed.)

A number of studies conducted at different times and in different locations have provided evidence that corroborates the findings of Wolfgang (e.g., MacDonald, 1961). Former Attorney General Ramsay Clark (1970), for example, has estimated that "two-thirds of all aggravated assaults occur within a family or among neighbors or friends," and Amir (1971) has reported that rape is most often committed by someone acquainted with his victim.

These features of crime point to the importance of causes of violence which are more or less independent of the personality of the offender. We will now examine them in terms of the situational conditions that underlie them.

The Role of Situational Factors in Violence

Motives

According to some, mostly psychoanalytic, observers, while the motives behind homicide may seem trivial, they are actually a disguise for some more deeply rooted cause. Others have seen in the trivial motives evidence for the accumulation of frustrations; they have argued that an insult or minor threat could not actually be considered the cause of so serious an event. They say that the offenders have been carrying with them a reservoir of earlier frustrations which, added to the minor insult or threat, become too much for them to bear. Still others have suggested that what may seem minor insults and threats to outside observers may in fact be perceived as major assaults to the offender's self-esteem. All of these explanations have in common a focus on some internal characteristic of the offender. However, rather than examining personality dynamics in an attempt to explain why minor events trigger homicide, a more fruitful search can be conducted by examining other environmental variables which are present in the homicide situation.

Victim-Offender Relationships: The Role of Similarity and Familiarity in Violence

The most outstanding feature of Wolfgang's analysis is the many ways in which familiarity and similarity manifest themselves. Offenders and victims are most likely to be familiar with one another prior to the homicide; the homicide is most likely to occur in a place familiar to the offender; the weapon is usually familiar to the offender. The most intimate, familiar relationship that two people can share—marriage—accounted not only for a large proportion of all homicides, but also tended to be the victim-offender relationship that contained the most violence and brutality. Rape also tends to occur in an environment familiar to the offender, against a victim familiar to the offender (Amir, 1971). Even the looting of stores during a riot will most likely take place in those establishments with which the looters are most familiar (Berk & Aldrich, 1972).

The most striking implication of these findings is that people with whom one interacts most often in a positive, even loving, manner are also those toward whom one may interact most violently. This leads us to the idea that there may be something in the nature of close relationships (other than the mere fact that friends spend more time in contact with each other than with strangers) which increases the probability that aggression will occur.

You Sometimes Hurt the One You Love.   A hypothesis may be proposed that as a person becomes increasingly familiar with another, the probability that he or she will aggress against the other will also increase. Although the statistics generated by Wolfgang, Amir, and others, bear this out, no satisfactory explanation for this effect has been provided.

There are a number of possible explanations for the finding that aggression is more probable toward a familiar victim. According to an interpretation based on the psychoanalytic school, the formation of positive emotional bonds with another involves giving up some autonomy and freedom; the stronger the positive bonds, the more individuality must be sacrificed. Therefore, relationships between people tend to be ambivalent, and the extent of ambivalence is directly related to the amount of attraction they feel toward one another. As the positive affect between two people increases, so does the negative affect. If positive interaction between the two is fairly intense, negative interaction, as during an argument, will be equally strong. In other words, the *intensity* of interaction between any two people is relatively constant, while the *quality* of the affect, positive or negative, changes with the circumstances. For example, positive interaction with a recent acquaintance might involve a handshake, a smile, and some casual conversation, while negative interaction with the same person might take the form of a mild insult or sneer. With a close friend or relative, however, positive interaction generally involves sharing secrets or objects and close physical contact. When one wishes to express disapproval of such a person, it will be done in an intense fashion, as by a strong verbal attack or by physical injury.

Another explanation may be given in terms of the principles proposed earlier: the familiarity-aggression effect can be seen as a conflict of values and norms. Nearly everyone in Western society learns contradictory norms and values for assertion and aggression and for self-control and restraint. In the presence of familiar others (or in a familiar physical environment), people act less defensively and do not censor their behavior to the extent that they do in the presence of strangers (or in unfamiliar surroundings). In other words, people are more likely to act impulsively and are less likely to inhibit themselves in the presence of close friends and relatives. Therefore, given a relatively mild provocation, people are more apt to respond aggressively toward friends than toward strangers, and in a familiar than an unfamiliar setting.

It is also possible that in familiar places a mild insult or threat will seem greater than it would otherwise. This can be due to the fact that a familiar environment, by virtue of its familiarity, does not intrude very much on a person's consciousness; there are few if any novel features in a familiar environment to hold one's attention. A mild insult may be exaggerated because it stands out from the relatively unobtrusive environment. In a novel environment, the insult may seem less intense since it must compete with other novel features of the environment for attention.

Not only are people more likely to aggress in familiar environments, but they are more likely to take actions of any kind. In research on altruism, it has been found that people were more quick to help a person in distress in familiar than in

unfamiliar environments (Latané & Darley, 1970). In terms of
the aggression model presented in Chapter 1, these results suggest that pro-helping norms will be acted upon more quickly
in a familiar environment because inhibitory, anti-helping norms
are relatively weak in such situations.

Even though it is possible to explain why crimes of violence
are more likely against friends and relatives than strangers, and
why such crimes tend to be more brutal than those committed
against others, it is difficult to imagine how people who are normally affectionate toward one another can, in a relatively short
time, become violent and brutal. In order to resolve this paradox it will be necessary to examine some of the cognitive dynamics that may operate in aggressive encounters.

The Cognitive Consequences of Aggressing.   When we are familiar and friendly with others, we develop positive attitudes
toward them and expect our interactions with them to be plea-
surable and psychologically rewarding. When such people anger,
insult, or disappoint us, one of our initial impulses is likely to
be aggression or retaliation. Therefore, when we are provoked
by our friends, a conflict is experienced between our normally
favorable attitudes and behaviors toward them and aggressive
tendencies toward them.

This is a difficult conflict to resolve. After all, we would not
become friendly or intimate with people who were not pleasing
to us. When they anger or otherwise provoke us, we have to
weigh the consequences of our aggressive tendencies against
the long-range effects such aggression might have. We may wish
to hurt them in retaliation, but at the same time not lose their
friendship. In most such situations, the conflict is resolved by
nonviolent means: the individual decides either that aggression
would be too costly or inappropriate or that his or her positive
feelings toward the other person outweigh the immediately felt
negative feelings. In some cases, however, the conflict is resolved by violent means. Aggression is most apt to be used in
such a situation when the person provoked is in a familiar environment or has a weapon readily at hand.

Let us assume that aggression has already occurred, that Person A has aggressed against his friend, Person B. At this point, there still may be some residual conflict, wherein A retains in his mind positive feelings toward B. Having already aggressed, A must now justify his actions to himself. He is likely to reevaluate B, adding reasons to justify his (A's) aggression and minimizing his feelings of friendliness toward B. (Likewise, if, in such a conflict situation, the individual decides not to aggress even though he may be provoked, he will also think of justifications for this decision. Because of this justification, it is not unusual for verbal disagreements to end in a reconciliation in which both parties feel closer to one another than prior to the dispute. This emotional arousal and its reinterpretation is discussed by Zillmann 1979, 1984).

When aggression occurs there is a general tendency to devalue the victim of the attack. This devaluation may be successful enough to warrant even further attacks, each with attendant devaluations of the victim. In this way, a general increase in the amount or intensity of aggression will occur. The paradox of inordinate amounts of violence being perpetrated against friends and relatives can be resolved by recognizing the need of the aggressor to justify his or her actions, usually by devaluing the victim (Bandura, Underwood, & Fromson, 1975; Lerner, 1980). Those victims requiring the greatest amounts of devaluation are friends and relatives, and those provocations which necessitate maximum devaluation of the victim tend to be the trivial ones. With successful devaluation, additional amounts of violence become easier to administer (Goldstein, Davis, & Herman, 1975). Victims, too, justify the aggression administered to them by thinking up reasons for their victimization. These include devaluing themselves and attributing the causes of the aggressor's actions to some characteristic or flaw in themselves. Being a victim of violence also reduces the victim's trust in others generally (Berglas, 1985).

The consequences of devaluation of the victim are far-reaching. On an international level, nations devalue enemies in times of war; within societies, the poor and the jobless, the sick and the needy are frequently devalued. Melvin Lerner (1970, 1980) has proposed a theory on the psychological devaluation of victims of circumstance which he calls the "just world phenomenon." According to Lerner, people have a need to believe that events in the world are not unjust, fortuitous, meaningless, or random, but that things happen as a result of some orderly and logical process of causality. The need to believe that the world is an orderly place leads to some surprising inferences. If the world is orderly, then things happen to people because of their own efforts. The Protestant ethic clearly implies this. Therefore, good things should not happen to people who are bad, nor should bad things happen to those who are good. Most people probably think of themselves as honest, righteous, and moral, and when material or psychological ills befall them, it is difficult for them to understand. After all, bad things should not happen to them since they do not consider themselves deserving of "punishment." The most common prayer is probably "Why me?" (followed closely by "What have I done to deserve this?").

If we observe good or bad things happening to others there is a tendency to look for explanations; and if people look hard enough, they will find—or fabricate—them. Reasons and causes for events serve to strengthen belief in the justness and orderliness of the world. The unemployed are seen as out of work because they are "lazy"; slum-dwellers live in rundown housing because they are "sloppy"; the poor have too many children because they are "oversexed"; women are raped because they wear immodest clothing. All of these "explanations" serve to sustain the belief that the world is just. People, in other words, not only are believed to get what they deserve but also to deserve what they get.

An experiment by Jones and Aronson (1973) found that the more respectable the victim of a rape, the greater the fault attributed to her for the incident. College students were presented with a description of a rape, the victim being described either as a virgin, as married, or as divorced. When asked how much they considered the rape to be the fault of the victim, students attributed greatest fault to the married woman and least to the divorced woman. These results suggest that it is more difficult to understand and justify the rape of a married woman or a virgin, and in order to maintain their beliefs in a just world, the subjects of the study assigned the greatest responsibility to these victims.

When we observe a victim of violence, there is a tendency to justify his or her victimization, no less so if we are the perpetrators of that violence. If we aggress against someone, particularly if it is difficult to justify such aggression, there will be a tendency to devalue the victim, to attribute fault to the victim for our own acts of aggression. One area in which this can be seen is in family violence.

Family Violence and the Metamorphosis of Aggression

Because violence in the family takes place behind closed doors, the precise extent of child and spouse abuse is unknown. It has been estimated that between 1.8 million and 5.7 million American couples annually experience violence (Straus, Gelles, & Steinmetz, 1979) and that each year between 200,000 and 2 million children are physically abused by their parents (Gelles, 1980). In a nationwide survey Gil (1970) found that the median child abuse rate for the United States as a whole was approximately 4.4 children per 100,000, but the rate is probably greater because family violence incidents often go unreported to the authorities.

Is violence in the family increasing? We certainly read and hear more about wife abuse and child abuse today than we did 5 or 10 years ago. This gives the impression that the incidence and prevalence of family violence are increasing. We may simply have become less tolerant of family violence in recent years and are therefore more concerned about it; this concern gives rise to increased media attention to the topic. Not so long ago, nothing that occurred within the confines of one's home was considered anyone else's business. Parents felt free to rear their children as they wished, and many husbands believed that a marriage license was also a hitting license. Since the mid-1960s family violence has come to be perceived as a social problem, demanding the attention of social and law enforcement agencies. It may be that our attitudes toward family violence have changed and not its incidence. The fact is that without statistics on family violence over a long period of time we have no way of knowing whether there has been any change in its occurrence.

There have been two types of research on child and spouse abuse. The first attempts to identify the personality characteristics and unique experiences of abusers (or of victims!) (Parke & Collmer, 1975; Rosenbaum & O'Leary, 1981; Spinetta & Rigler, 1972). These studies have not been very productive for the same reasons that attempts to identify "criminal types," which were discussed in Chapter 2, have not been successful. The research on characteristics of abusive parents and spouses suggests that those who engage in child and spouse abuse are not very different psychologically from normal, nonabusing parents and spouses. In his national survey, Gill (1970) found that over 58 percent of his respondents agreed with the statement that "almost anybody could at some time injure a child in his care," and over 22 percent agreed that they themselves "could at some time injure a child." In a study of 60 abusing parents, Steele and Pollock (1968) noted: "If all the people we studied were gathered together, they would not seem much different than a group picked by stopping the first dozen people one would meet on a downtown street" (p. 106).

One finding from this research has entered the public consciousness—children who are abused grow up to be abusive parents. There is some truth to this belief. In his nationwide study, Gelles (1980) found that 18.5 percent of his respondents who stated that their mothers had hit them more than twice a year reported using severe violence toward their own children during the year of the survey. This rate is more than 50 percent greater than the rate for respondents who experienced physical punishment less than twice a year. Physical punishment by fathers made less difference. Respondents whose fathers hit them more than twice had a violence rate of 16.7 percent, while the rate for respondents whose fathers hit them less than twice was 13.2 percent. The act of observing violence in the family, such as parents hitting each other, rather than being the target of violence, is strongly related to using severe punishment toward one's own children (Carroll, 1977). Nevertheless, this intergenerational transmission of family violence still does not account for the majority of child or spouse abuse. Most abusive family members were not themselves abused as children.

A second research strategy has been to look at social and situational factors that contribute to family violence (Green, 1980; Herrenkohl, Herrenkohl, & Egolf, 1983; Parke & Collmer, 1975). These studies examine such variables as stress and power in the family (Gelles, 1980) and the situational antecedents of violence (Dobash & Dobash, 1984).

In their review of theories of family violence, Gelles and Straus (1979) conclude that an adequate theory would include social learning and the role of situational and structural aspects of the family. This is generally the approach we have taken throughout this book. With respect to the dynamics of family violence, this approach suggests that a necessary condition of child abuse, for example, is a parent who has learned a repertoire of aggressive responses. Second, the parent must experience conflict about aggressing toward the child. Some provocation to aggress must be salient along with long-standing positive feelings toward the child. The third step is the decision to strike the child. This will be accompanied by cognitive devaluation of the child, justifying still further aggression. As the violence escalates, the parent becomes less reflective and self-conscious about what it is he or she is doing (playing the role of a parent punishing a child) and begins to focus exclusively on the feelings associated with hitting.

Interviews with battered wives (Dobash & Dobash, 1984; Goldstein, 1980) suggest some of the dynamics of spouse abuse. The initial instance of physical assault against a woman tends to occur when the husband has been drinking and an argument around sexual jealousy or about domestic matters arises. The violence is followed by the husband's apologies and profession of love for his wife. Two types of escalation of violence then occur. First, there is an increase in the overall frequency and severity of assaults. While the interval between the first violent episode and the second may be weeks or months, the time between the second and third episode will be shorter, and continues to decrease between succeeding incidents. This is one reason it is so difficult to terminate a violent relationship: at first it is an anomaly, an event out of the ordinary, for which the offender and the victim make excuses. Only after repeated instances of abuse does the violence come to characterize the relationship. After having lived with the violence for some time, hidden from friends and relatives, and either ignored or excused it, the victim finds seeking help or leaving particularly difficult. A second type of escalation of aggression occurs within each violent episode: aggression begins at a low level and increases in severity throughout the episode.

If there do not appear to be psychological or social traits that clearly distinguish abusive parents or spouses from their non-abusive counterparts, perhaps the dynamic aspects of aggression involved in family violence are typical of aggression in general. To study these ideas, a series of experiments was conducted by Goldstein, Roger Davis, and their colleagues (Goldstein, Davis, & Herman, 1975; Goldstein, Davis, Kernis, & Cohn, 1981). The first experiment involved pairs of college students, one of whom was to reward or punish the other for responses on a learning task. Some students could punish the other with any of 10 verbal statements, ranging from mild ("That's no good") to strong ("Stupid son of a bitch") each time the learner made a mistake. Other students could use any of 10 levels of reward, ranging from mild ("Yes") to strong

("That's fantastic!") for correct answers to the learning task. Each of the students administered 20 rewards or 20 punishments to the learner. Following the learning task, the "teachers" were asked to evaluate the learners on cooperativeness, likeability, and intelligence. We expected that the subjects would find it increasingly easy to give severe verbal punishments to the learner as the experiment progressed. We also expected that this increased punishment would be accompanied by a general devaluation of the learner. This is precisely what we found. As students administered verbal punishments to the learner, the intensity of the punishment increased. In addition, subjects who punished the learner rated him significantly less cooperative, friendly, and likeable than those who rewarded the learner.[1] These findings have been replicated by others (Felson, 1982; Jaffe, Shapir, & Yinon, 1981; Potegal, 1979; see also Konečni & Ebbesen, 1976).

In a second experiment, some learners (who were accomplices of the experimenters) improved their learning performance as the study progressed, while other learners did not improve. Again, half the subjects in the experiment could reward the learner with varying degrees of reward for correct answers on the learning task, while the remaining half could punish the learner with varying degrees of verbal punishment for errors on the task. Regardless of the performance of the learner, subjects gave increasingly intense punishment to the learner as the learning task progressed. The results of this study are shown in Figure 3.1. Several attempts to inhibit escalation met uniformly with failure. In a series of studies (Goldstein, Davis, Kernis, & Cohn, 1981) we attempted to increase the subjects' self-consciousness (for example, by videotaping their performance or by leading them to believe they would later meet with their "victim"). Nevertheless, escalation of punishment continued unabated. In one study we provided subjects with a telephone

1. It should be noted that those subjects who rewarded correct responses also showed an escalation, giving increasing intensity of reward as the learning task progressed. See also Davis, Rainey, and Brock (1976).

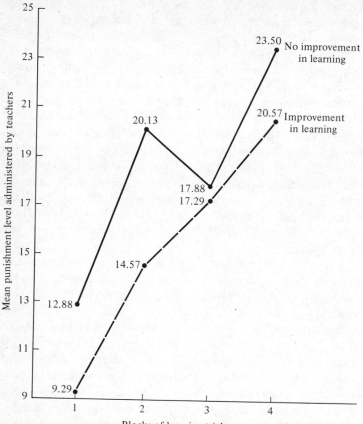

Figure 3.1 Escalation of aggression. (Adapted from Goldstein, Davis, and Herman.)

"hot line" that could be used to summon the experimenter. This significantly reduced the overall level of aggression (although escalation still occurred).

These experiments suggest, first, that normal people can become quite punitive with little or no apparent provocation, second, that it becomes increasingly easy to escalate the level of verbal aggression, third, that increasing verbal aggression is often accompanied by a general devaluation of the "victim," finally, these behaviors were found to occur regardless of the performance of the learner. This last finding suggests that once aggression is underway, it may operate in a fairly automatic fashion, independently of the behavior of the victim. This finding has also been reported in other research (Kipnis, Castell, Gergen, & Mauch, 1976; Zimbardo, 1969). It is not surprising in view of these results that following an argument or fight, the participants often cannot remember what the dispute was about. At some point the act of arguing or aggressing becomes autonomous and is done for its own sake. One reason for this may be that highly intense verbal or physical assault becomes self-reinforcing and may have an almost hypnotic effect wherein the actor loses awareness of his or her surroundings.

The "Weapons Effect"

Between 1963 and 1973, while the war in Vietnam was taking 46,121 American lives, guns here at home were responsible for 84,644 civilian deaths. Since the beginning of this century some 750,000 people have been killed in the United States by privately owned guns, 30 percent more than in all the wars in which this country has been involved in its entire history (Morris & Hawkins, 1970).

America is a heavily armed nation (though not the most heavily armed; see McPhee, 1984). Nearly one-half of all American homes have at least one lethal weapon, and there are an estimated 90 million firearms in the hands of civilians. In 1983, there were nearly 2,000 accidental deaths from firearms, 8,200 homicides, 183,000 robberies, and 165,000 aggravated assaults. Nearly three-fourths of the law enforcement officers killed each year are shot to death.

The homicide rates in those states with strict gun-control

laws are significantly lower than in those states with weak gun laws. Likewise, homicides and suicides by firearms are significantly lower in those countries with strict gun laws than in those without strict laws.

There are a number of ways in which the presence of weapons can lead to increased violence. A well-known and controversial experiment by L. Berkowitz and A. LePage (1967) of the University of Wisconsin found that the mere presence of a weapon during an aggression experiment could intensify the level of electric shock that subjects would administer to another person. Berkowitz has stated that "guns not only permit violence, they can stimulate it as well. The finger pulls the trigger, but the trigger may also be pulling the finger." The possession of a weapon, even though its owner is reluctant to use it, may increase the intensity of other forms of violence (Berkowitz & Frodi, 1977; Leyens & Parke, 1975; Turner, Simons, Bercowitz, & Frodi; see also Buss, Booker, & Buss, 1972; Page & Scheidt, 1971). In a society in which so many people are armed, the assumption that an opponent may be carrying a weapon often leads to the notion that it is better to "shoot first and ask questions later." As Morris and Hawkins (1970) have stated, "it is most implausible to assume that the individuals involved in the majority of murder cases are persons so determined to kill that in the absence of guns they will either seek to achieve that purpose with any available alternative or deliberately evade whatever restrictive gun legislation may be enacted. . . . Without the vehicle there is every reason to expect the violence to be both less lethal and less injurious" (p. 67). This issue is further discussed in Chapter 5.

Effects of Physiological Arousal

Any behavior requires a certain amount of physical energy to perform. If a person has already decided to aggress, the more energy he or she has available (that is, the more aroused the person is), the more intense will be the aggression.[2] An increasing number of studies indicates that a rise in arousal level usually leads to an increase in aggression, at least among those who are required to aggress as part of their experimental participation (Rule & Nesdale, 1976; Tannenbaum, 1971). In these studies it seems to make little difference whether the source of arousal is due to injected adrenaline (O'Neal & Kaufman, 1972), to sexually stimulating pictures (Barclay & Haber, 1965; Goldstein, Rosnow, Raday, Silverman, & Gaskell, 1975; Zillmann, 1971, 1984), to increased emotionality or frustration (Berkowitz, 1960; Buss, 1963; Feierabend & Feierabend, 1966), or to unpleasant arousing noise (Geen & O'Neal, 1969).

Sex and Violence

The evidence is strongest for the relationship between sexual arousal and aggression; an increase in sexual arousal is generally followed by an increase in aggressiveness. Barclay (1971), for example, found that subjects who were sexually aroused became more aggressive following their arousal, but that those who were aroused as a result of a slapstick comedy film did not become more aggressive.[3] A possible reason why there is a close relationship between sex and aggression is the fact that the brain centers capable of evoking sexual and aggressive behaviors are located anatomically close to one another. Hence, stimulation of one area may result in stimulation of adjacent areas. Another reason, based loosely on psychoanalytic theory, is the fact that both sexual and aggressive behaviors are closely regulated by society (Freud, 1930; Moyer, 1971b).

2. This will be true providing the amount of energy is not so high as to be debilitating.
3. Research subjects in many of these studies are required by the experimenter to act aggressively. There has been no research on whether sexually aroused persons show an increased *desire* to behave aggressively. There is some evidence that those who have committed violence are more easily sexually aroused than nonviolent persons (Farley & Farley, 1972; Kercher & Walker, 1973; Sapolsky, 1984).

Seymour Feshbach (1980) has noted that:

> many researchers interpret the sexual facilitation of aggression within the framework of an arousal effect. I don't think that's an adequate explanation. Sex and aggression are not *arbitrarily* related. There's a reason why, in our society, people censor violence and censor sex. In general, in animals, there are close hormonal and physiological connections. I would say at the human level there is a connection, but it is not an inevitable one. It comes from socialization. Both sex and aggression get socialized in our society with strong taboo connotations. So it is this common taboo quality that joins them together. The way I would interpret the research we've done so far is that a sexually-arousing stimulus is presented and an increase in aggression is obtained. It's not because the stimulus aroused the person, it's because of weakened inhibitions, so that now it becomes "appropriate" to engage in another inhibited response. (p. 275)

Feshbach also noted that "when sex is accompanied by embarrassment, guilt, and conflict, you get strong arousal but a decrement in aggressive behavior." Research bears this out. Among individuals who are self-conscious or who experience anxiety, sexual arousal may inhibit rather than facilitate aggression (Baron, 1974; Frodi, 1977).

In American culture, sex and aggression are often presented in tandem, not merely during the socialization process, where prohibitions on sexual and aggressive expression are taught, but in films, magazines, and television programs. In many forms of popular entertainment attractive young women are portrayed as victims of violence. As a result of classical conditioning a portion of the audience is apt to associate women with violence. Research by Malamuth and Donnerstein (1984) demonstrates that it is the violence in erotic films, rather than their sexual content, that contributes to increased aggression toward women.

Alcohol, Drugs, and Aggression

The degree to which alcohol is present in incidents of human violence is, to coin a phrase, staggering. In the United States and elsewhere, homicides and other violent crimes are most often committed by offenders while "under the influence" of alcohol. Wolfgang (1958) found that of 588 cases of criminal homicide, alcohol was present in at least 64 percent of them, and he reports the results of other studies indicating a strong relationship between alcohol and violent crime in England, Norway, and Yugoslavia. Shupe (1954) reported that 91 of 100 people arrested for assault or for carrying a concealed weapon showed evidence of alcohol intake.

Experimental studies with human subjects on the effects of alcohol on aggression do not always lead to consistent results. Bennett, Buss, and Carpenter (1969) gave their research subjects varying quantities of vodka and found no differences in aggressiveness with changes in vodka dosage. On the other hand, Shuntich and Taylor (1972) found that subjects drunk on bourbon were significantly more aggressive than those given no drugs or a placebo.

If there is a relationship between alcohol and aggression it is not necessarily a linear one. Peeke, Ellman, and Herz (1973) placed male convict cichlid fish in tanks with .07, .18, or .33 percent ethanol. After several hours, another male cichlid in a glass tube was suspended in the tank. Attacks were most ferocious and more frequent among fish in the 18 percent solution. A curvilinear relationship between alcohol dosage and hostility was noted among male college students by Kreutzer, Schneider, and Myatt (1984).

To understand the effects of alcohol and other drugs it is important to keep in mind that we are socialized into their use, effects, and cultural meaning. The effects which they have are in part determined by the expectations of the user. Alcohol is medically classified as a depressant that inhibits activity of the central nervous system. This inhibition is both physiological and cognitive. In Western society alcohol is often used as a stimulant (a "pick-me-up") and as a social lubricant. That a drug which dulls the senses can be perceived as heightening sensitivity points to the importance of expectations in drug effects. Americans are apt to become more hostile with moderate alcohol consumption. Among the Irish, whose per capita consumption of alcohol is high, lethal violence "under the influence" is rare.

Alcohol may not in itself influence aggression. Rather, our *expectations* about alcohol may be the deciding factor. Marlatt and his colleagues (Marlatt, Kosturn, & Lang, 1975; Marlatt & Rohsenow, 1981) compared the behavior of people who actually drank liquor (vodka and tonic) with the behavior of those who only *thought* they drank liquor (but only drank tonic). Those who believed they had been drinking vodka were more belligerent than those who had actually been drinking but did not believe so. These and other studies (e.g., Critchlow, 1983; Kreutzer, Schneider, & Myatt, 1984) suggest that the link between alcohol and aggression is not primarily a physiological one but a social one.

This social link between alcohol and aggression may apply to other drugs as well. In a study af marijuana users, Becker (1953) found that juveniles' expectations about the effects of the drug determined its effects. If they expected marijuana to enhance their arousal, they became more agitated, whereas if they expected marijuana to act as a depressant, they became more placid.

Most drugs that are widely consumed have little direct effect on aggressive behavior. A 1979 survey of state prisoners found that among violent offenders only robbers among the inmate population had a relatively high proportion (38 percent) who said they had been under the influence of drugs, and most of these said they had smoked marijuana (U.S. Department of Justice, 1983). In a review of drug effects (Tinklenberg & Stillman, 1970) it was noted that marijuana, LSD, mescaline, psilocybin, heroin, morphine, opium, codeine, methadone, and the barbiturates did not uniformly lead to an increase in aggressiveness. Of all the drugs reviewed, only amphetamines and alcohol were found to be related to an increase in aggression.

We might propose, along with Tavris (1982), that alcohol and other drugs are an *excuse* for aggression rather than its cause. A husband may drink in order to abuse his spouse and absolve himself of responsibility, blaming his behavior on the alcohol.

"Old Times There Are Not Forgotten"

Where you live is apt to determine how aggressive you are. The rate of violent crime is significantly greater in the southern United States than in the northern states (see Table 3.3). In 1983 the homicide rate in southern states was 10.4 per 100,000 and ranged from 6.4 to 8.5 per 100,000 for other regions of the country.

Gastil (1971) proposed that the higher rate of violence in the American South is due to its cultural tradition of violence: people more often carry weapons, attempt to redress insults to personal honor, and only infrequently receive punishment for such "honorable" violence. By tracing migration patterns of southerners to nonsouthern states, Gastil was able to account for a significant portion of the homicide rates of all states. The homicide rate for any given state is highly related to the proportion of southerners or descendants of southerners in the state's population, although other factors, such as education and income, also account for variations in the homicide rate (Erlanger, 1976).

TABLE 3.3   U.S. Crime Rate by Region, 1983
(rate per 100,000 population)

	North-eastern States	North Central States	Southern States	Western States
Murder	6.8	6.4	10.4	8.5
Forcible rape	26.0	31.0	34.4	44.4
Robbery	313.9	166.2	171.2	240.5
Aggravated assault	250.5	212.6	303.7	323.3

Source: Federal Bureau of Investigation, *Uniform Crime Reports,* 1983.

Deindividuation

There are characteristics of the environment, such as crowding
and temperature extremes, which are often thought to influence
aggression by first elevating the individual's level of physiological arousal. These studies are discussed later in this chapter
(see "The Physical Environment"). Philip Zimbardo (1969)
and others (Diener, 1976, 1977) have suggested that the effects
of environmental stressors, such as crowding, may influence the
individual's feelings of identity or anonymity and that this might
account for changes in aggression. Individuals in densely or
heavily populated places may feel less unique, less visible, and
as a result, less accountable for their actions. The loss of self-
consciousness and the accompanying feeling of anonymity is referred to as *deindividuation*. Deindividuated people behave
more impulsively and violently than they would under other
circumstances.

A test of the effects of deindividuation on aggression was
conducted by Watson (1973). Based on deindividuation theory
he hypothesized that soldiers who wear disguising battle dress
commit more atrocities in time of war than those who do not
mask their appearance. Changes in appearance may be accomplished by body or face painting, wearing special garments or
masks, or hair cutting. In cultures where such changes in appearance occur, combatants should feel relatively deindividuated; they should not feel identifiable or distinctive or be highly
aware of their uniqueness. To test this hypothesis, Watson used
information contained in the Human Relations Area Files, a
repository of data on the world's cultures. He obtained data
concerning physical appearance during battle and the extremity of violence in warfare on 23 cultures. Extremity of aggression was measured by the extent to which torture and mutila-
tion of enemies was carried out and the extent to which prisoners
were executed. The results are summarized in Table 3.4. As
predicted, excessive aggression was employed significantly more
often in cultures where changes in physical appearance pre-

TABLE 3.4   Relationship Between Changes in Physical
Appearance Prior to Battle and Extremity of Aggression in Warfare

	- Deindividuation	
	Changed Appearance	Unchanged Appearance
Aggressive	12	1
Nonaggressive	3	7

Note: Entries are number of cultures in each category. $\chi^2 = 7.12$; $df = 1$; $p < .01$.

Source: Adapted from "Investigation into Deindividuation Using a Cross-cultural Survey Technique," by R. I. Watson, Jr., 1973, *Journal of Personality and Social Psychology, 25,* 342–345. Copyright © 1973 by the American Psychological Association. Used by permission.

ceded battle than in those cultures where no change in appearance was made.

Anger and Aggression

Emotions generally, and anger in particular, are frequently thought to be closely related to aggression. The precise definition of an emotion is one of the long-standing debates in psychology and one of the most interesting (Lazarus, Coyne, & Folkman, 1982; Plutchik & Kellerman, 1980; Zajonc, 1980). Psychologists' views of emotion have changed from time to time. At the beginning of this century an emotion was believed to be a psychophysiological and purely subjective event. With the rise of behaviorism, it was considered a learned response. In the 1970s, cognitive theories of emotion predominated. A new view has developed in the past few years, social constructivism, in which an emotion is seen as a rule-governed social role. James Averill (1982, 1983) and Carol Tavris (1982) have applied this approach to anger.

A number of theories, including biological, psychoanalytic, and learning theories, propose that anger is a cause of, or a necessary condition for, aggression. And indeed, in the experiences of many individuals, anger *is* a cause of their aggression (Averill, 1983). But is aggression an automatic, biological response to the experience of anger? If so, why are there cultural variations in people's responses to anger? For example, the Mbuti of Zaire use humor and ridicule in response to anger (Tavris, 1982), and there are some cultures in which people do not experience anger at all (Montagu, 1978).

In our culture, anger gives rise to aggression because we have learned that aggression is permissible, or at least more acceptable, if it follows anger. Like the effects of sexual arousal, alcohol, and drugs on aggression, anger leads to aggression among those who believe that anger leads to aggression. And like alcohol, anger provides an excuse for one's aggression. It allows husbands to beg forgiveness from their wives, to disclaim responsibility for their actions, in fact, to lay the blame on their wives, who gave rise to the anger in the first place.

We are exposed in this culture to what Tavris calls the "anger industry," those psychiatrists, social scientists, and laypeople—armed with foam-rubber bats and primal screams—urging us to express our anger. They argue that bottling up anger is a cause of depression, hypertension, obesity, heart disease, and ulcers. There is little empirical support for any of these beliefs (Tavris, 1982). Among Japanese-Americans, for example, who traditionally do not vent their anger, the incidence of heart disease is very low. It is perhaps more likely that depression, obesity, and illness give rise to anger than the other way around.

> In many pop-psych discussions of the danger of suppressed anger, the content of the anger is regarded as less important than what we do with it. This mistaken emphasis ignores the lessons of history, anthropology, and Freud, all of which show that sometimes suppressed anger makes social life possible. (Tavris, 1982, p. 119)

The Physical Environment

All behavior occurs in time and place, and there is mounting evidence that the physical environment plays an important role in the type of behavior that occurs. The effects of the physical environment on aggression and crime have been examined in two ways, first, by studying the effects of the constructed environment, and second, of the natural environment.

The Constructed Environment and Crime

Since the ground-breaking work of Jeffery (1971, 1977) and Newman (1972) on crime and the physical environment, there has been increasing attention by criminologists to the geophysical distribution of crimes (e.g., Brantingham & Brantingham, 1981). This research, instead of looking for the motives that underlie crime, assumes that there is a motivated individual intent on committing a crime. It then seeks to explain the particular type of crime that occurs or the particular target chosen by the offender. For example, a study by David and Scott (1973) compared crime in the cities of Toledo, Ohio, which has a high rate of larceny, burglary, and auto theft, with crime in Rosario, Argentina, which has a high rate of assault and rape. David and Scott suggest that in Toledo shoplifting is made easy by the physical layout of supermarkets, and the burglary rate is high because residential homes are isolated from one another (see also Brown & Altman, 1981, on choice of burglary sites). In Rosario, homes and businesses are intermixed, thereby minimizing the opportunity and temptation to commit burglary. On the other hand, opportunities for sexual and personal assaults are great in Rosario because of the high amount of personal contact among people.

Yancey (1972) has analyzed the relationship between architectural design and violent crime in the once-heralded and now demolished Pruitt-Igoe housing project in St. Louis. Isolated doors, apartments, stairways, and elevators and the arrangement of living units to prevent the development of informal social controls and surveillance were among the reasons cited for the high crime rate. In a study of juvenile delinquency in France, the best predictor of future delinquency was simply whether a youth lived in a building of six stories or more (Peyreffitte, 1982). If constructed features of the environment can give rise to violence and crime, then alterations of the environment might mitigate crime. In Chapter 5 we discuss studies on changes in the environment and reduction of crime.

The Natural Environment

For generations we have known that cities have higher rates of crime and violence than small towns (Burgess, 1916). This is true not only in the United States, but in nearly every country for which crime statistics are available (Archer & Gartner, 1984b). The rates for five violent crimes in urban, suburban, and rural areas of the United States are shown in Table 3.5. In each case, the rate of crime is greatest in urban areas. To what features of the city can we attribute these greater rates of violence and crime? Among the answers offered, we have already explored deindividuation and the urban dweller's greater chronic arousal resulting from excessive social stimulation. Additional

TABLE 3.5   U.S. Crime Rate by City Size (crime victimization rate per 100,000 persons age 12 or older)

	Urban	Suburban	Rural
Rape and attempted rape	135	93	63
Robbery	497	177	83
Aggravated assault	1340	875	746
Simple assault	2169	1727	1358
Personal larceny (with contact)	685	260	91

Note: Data are based on a 1981 crime victimization survey.

Source: U.S. Department of Justice, Bureau of Justice Statistics.

research has examined the effects on aggression of crowding, population density, and temperature.

A series of well-known studies by J. B. Calhoun (1962) reported that rats reared in crowded conditions developed abnormal behavior patterns, including a deterioration in social and sexual behavior, increased infant mortality, and hyperaggressiveness. Freedman (1975) suggests that the presence of additional animals in these studies may intensify certain physiological responses and social interaction, which may account for the observed effects, at least in animals. The evidence that crowding per se increases aggression is inconclusive.

Researchers in this field distinguish between *population density,* which refers to the number of individuals in a given amount of space, and *crowding,* the subjective feeling that there are too many individuals in a given space. In his own research, Freedman (Freedman, Klevansky, & Ehrlich, 1971; Freedman, Levy, Buchanan, & Price, 1972) examined the behavioral and emotional effects of short-term population density on humans. The findings indicate no main effect for density on creativity, memory, performance of manual tasks, or aggressiveness. If one considers the sex of the subjects, however, a general heightening of emotion in densely populated spaces is found (Freedman, 1975; Ross, Layton, Erickson, & Schopler, 1973). Males, who are generally more aggressive than females, become more aggressive in densely populated spaces, whereas females become less agggressive. There does not appear to be any unidirectional effect of short-term population density on feelings of hostility or aggressiveness.

Zimbardo (1969) has suggested that individuals in large cities may feel anonymous or deindividuated, a state that increases their willingness to engage in antisocial acts. While there is evidence to support the contention that deindividuation increases aggression, there are no data indicating that urban residents feel less individuated than people in small towns. If deindividuation were responsible for the relatively high rate of urban violence, how could we explain the lack of violence in densely populated cities like Amsterdam and Tokyo? For example, in Tokyo, where population density is greater than in New York City, the 12 million residents commit fewer than 300 homicides per year, in contrast to New York City's nearly 2,000. Indeed, there is some evidence indicating that the severity of crime is greater when the offender is accompanied by another individual (thus making the offender more individuated) who is supportive of violence (Felson, Ribner, & Siegel, 1984).

One explanation of urban crime rates and the relatively greater rate of crime in high-rise buildings is based on citizens' feelings of community (e.g., Archer & Gartner, 1984b; Bynum & Purri, 1984; Shotland & Goodstein, 1984). Close personal interactions, which are more difficult to establish in cities and in high-rise buildings, may heighten people's sense of mutual responsibility and lessen the probability of at least certain types of crime (property crimes, especially).

Based on laboratory experiments, Robert Baron (1979) has proposed a curvilinear relationship between ambient temperature and human aggression. Up to a certain point (about 85 degrees Fahrenheit) increased temperature is related to increased aggression. Beyond that point, increases in temperature lead, not to more aggression, but to a singleminded effort to escape the heat.

If one examines actual crimes, rather than laboratory measures of hostility and aggression, increased temperatures appear to be linearly related to violent crimes (Anderson & Anderson, 1984). Even when temperatures approached the 100-degree mark, increases in homicide and rape were noted. There are numerous differences between laboratory studies of temperature and analyses of real-life crime, any of which might account for the discrepancy in findings. For example, high temperatures in a research laboratory are apt to be more obtrusive, while in the natural world high temperatures do not so often give rise to attempts merely to escape from their unpleasant effects.

In this chapter we have reviewed a number of direct and indirect precursors of violence and crime that lie outside the offender's personal makeup. While it is tempting to fix the blame for an antisocial act on the offender, it is likely in many cases to be due to largely fortuitous and impersonal characteristics of the physical and social environment. Of course, not everyone in the same physical setting will engage in the same behavior, and it is important to keep the role of social learning in mind. Yet I think it would be fair to say that much serious aggression is committed by individuals who are not distinctive in personality or temperament from their nonaggressive peers. The role that situational factors play in aggression and crime do not necessarily obviate the responsibility of criminal offenders for their actions, though this is more of a legal or moral issue than a psychological one.

4
Factors Associated with Nonaggression

Children in violence-torn Belfast, Northern Ireland, were asked to imagine that they had found a package on the street and to describe what was in it. In contrast to a comparable group of children in placid Edinburgh, Scotland, the Belfast children were more likely to think the package contained a bomb. (See Table 4.1.) What to the Edinburgh children were innocent, everyday items (milk bottles, letters, a pack of cigarettes) were to the Belfast children objects laden with danger (Jahoda & Harrison, 1975). The experience of violence changes even young children's perceptions of their environment.

A lack of experience with violence may in itself be sufficient to preclude aggressive behavior. In other cases, such as in Northern Ireland, even everyday objects may become aggression-provoking cues. In the absence of atypical physiological arousal, with no likely target of aggression and with no weapon near at hand, aggressive behavior is unlikely to occur. There are situations and processes, both internal and external to the individual, that minimize the likelihood of aggressive behavior. Before looking at such nonaggression variables, a closer exami-

TABLE 4.1   Number of Children Perceiving One or More
Common Objects as "Bombs"

	Bombs	Not Bombs
Age 6		
Belfast	9	21
Edinburgh	1	29
Age 10		
Belfast	24	6
Edinburgh	2	28

Source: From "Belfast Children: Some Effects of a Conflict Environment," by G. Jahoda and S. Harrison, 1975, Irish Journal of
Psychology, 1, 1–19. Used by permission.

nation of aggression conflict is made in order to see more clearly
how nonaggression factors operate within the larger framework
of aggression.

Aggression Conflict

The decision of whether or not to act aggressively is a complex
one. The aggression model proposed in Chapter 1 states that
aggression will ensue when the sum of the long-term and situational factors associated with aggression is stronger to the individual than the sum of long-term and situational factors associated with nonaggression. The individual in essence uses a
kind of cognitive arithmetic to determine which of the two sets
of competing behavioral tendencies is strongest, and his or her
actions reflect this cognitive assessment. This decision-making
process occurs quickly, probably in a second or two, and is
often not entirely conscious. In complexity and rapidity it is
not unlike the cognitive and perceptual processes involved in
reading this page.

In situations in which one side of the equation, either the

pro- or the anti-aggression side, is predominant, the behavior
in which the individual will engage is easily determined. However, when the balance of opposing forces is nearly even, the
individual must weigh more closely each aspect of the entire
situation. He must decide how angered or upset he really is,
how just or unjust aggression would be in that situation, the
likelihood of retaliation, how characteristic he believes aggressive behavior to be of his own personality, and so on. We have
seen that an individual is capable of distorting his perceptions
of the potential victim, and he is equally able to distort his
perceptions of any other aspect of a potential aggression situation. Therefore, while it is possible to determine somewhat objectively how most people view various provocations, victims,
and situations, it should be clear that these factors may be
weighted and evaluated differently by different people and that
the outcome is influenced by subjective, psychological factors.
In cases where the pro- and anti-aggression forces are felt by
the individual to be of roughly equal intensity, we can speak of

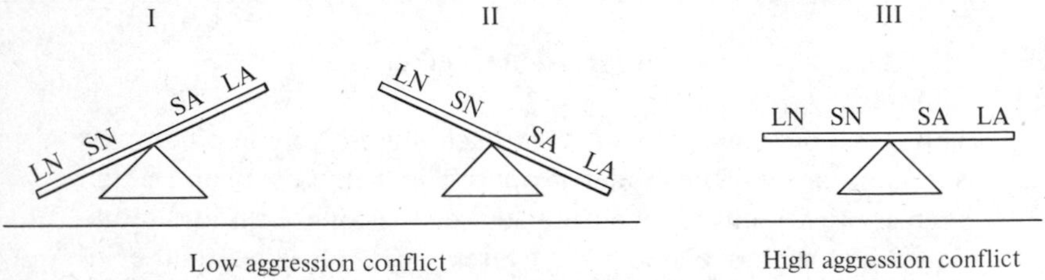

Low aggression conflict   High aggression conflict

Figure 4.1 Aggression conflict. In I the short-term and long-term
aggression factors are outweighed by the short-term and long-term
nonaggression factors, so nonaggressive behavior will result. In II,
the aggression factors outweigh the nonaggression factors, so aggression will result. In III, they about are equal, so it is unclear
which type of behavior will ultimately be expressed. In the last condition, the individual will have to evaluate closely each element in
the situation before deciding which behavior to engage in. (LN =
long-term nonaggression factors; SN = short-term nonaggression
factors; SA = short-term pro-aggression factors; LA = long-term
pro-aggression factors.)

a high-conflict situation. High-conflict situations require considerably more cognitive work to resolve than low-conflict situations simply because it is more difficult to justify one action over another. (See Figure 4.1.)

For some people aggression is never an easy behavior to justify; it is seen as morally wrong, inefficient, or unnecessary. For others aggression is seen as useful, appropriate, and rewarding. Just as there are two major classes of pro-aggression factors, so too are there two types of anti-aggression factors: long-term and situational. Long-term anti-aggression factors are more or less internalized, integrated features of an individual's personality and belief system. They include values, norms, attitudes, and moral principles which dictate against aggression, and also include the availability of nonaggressive strategies for resolving conflict.

Long-Term Nonaggression Factors

The most basic personality characteristic that could be associated with nonviolence is the individual's failure to acquire an aggressive repertoire in the first place. If people do not have a basic set of aggressive actions that can be used, they are unlikely to "improvise" or invent an aggressive response when a conflict arises. However, as we have seen, nearly everyone in Western society is exposed to aggressive models. Therefore in the discussions that follow it will be assumed that individuals have learned some aggressive behaviors and that, given some perceived provocation, they are potentially capable of violence. The question then becomes what factors might prevent aggression when some instigation is present.

The extent to which individuals learn aggression will help determine whether provocation is met with violence or with some other response. It will also determine whether and to what extent people are capable of being provoked. Those who are exposed to a variety of aggressive models will undoubtedly more extensive aggressive repertoires than people who y exposed to others' aggression. Those who live amidst are most likely to act violently upon (and often with only slight) provocation (Wolfgang & Ferracuti, 1967). On the other hand, people who rarely observe aggression in others are unlikely to act aggressively in any but the most extreme circumstances.

For any given individual, provocation may lead to aggression or to a number of nonaggressive responses, depending upon the strength of the provocation and the relative weighting of pro- and anti-aggression factors in the situation. For those who have in the past been rewarded for aggression, who have developed few inhibitions against aggression, and who have learned an extensive repertoire of aggressive behaviors, aggression will be a highly probable response. For those who have had little experience with aggression and have not been extensively exposed to aggressive models, aggression will be a fairly improbable response. Aggression becomes less probable when individuals are able to tolerate provocations well and are able to examine a situation from the point of view of other people. The different degrees of tolerance for frustration, anger, and fear which people acquire enable them to withstand different degrees of unpleasant experiences and emotional states before becoming physically assaultive. Furthermore, if an individual has learned a large number of alternative responses to provocation, aggression perhaps being one of these, he is more apt to use some nonaggressive response. In other words, the more alternative behaviors an individual can engage in, the less the probability that he will respond aggressively. There are a number of reasons that this is so. First, if an individual must choose one behavior from many possibilities, he must stop and decide which behavior to select. This process involves time and cognitive reflection, and therefore minimizes the chances of acting impulsively. Second, even if the person chooses a behavioral response at random, the more nonaggressive alternatives he has available, the less likely his choice will involve aggression.

The Evaluation of Behavior

After 6 years of marriage, Bill and Irene no longer get along well. Particularly after he has been drinking, Bill picks fights with Irene and afterwards accuses her of provoking him. "You know how I get when I've been drinking," he says, "so don't do anything to start a fight." Aggressors excuse their violence by blaming their victims, blaming the alcohol they have consumed, and even holding nebulous forces responsible: "I just lose control when I'm angry," says Bill. Are these merely prevarications, strategies for avoiding responsibility for his actions?

It is not only patterns of behavior that people learn at an early age, but also how to talk and think about behavior. Children learn what sorts of excuses and self-statements permit or justify aggression. They learn what aggressors say afterwards to explain their actions. They even learn which behaviors are to be considered aggressive in the first place. What, to the victim, is obviously an aggressive act may not be thought of as such by the aggressor or by a third party (Smith, 1983). Political terrorists, after bombing a public place, usually deny that they are aggressive and instead insist that the government is "the real criminal." The judgment that an action was aggressive depends on who is doing the aggressing, against whom, for what purpose, and with what effect. This is true of political terrorism (Schmid & de Graaf, 1982) as well as individual acts of aggression (Mummendey, 1984).

The labels we attach to actions, people, and situations are acquired through classical and operant conditioning and social learning. Children may hear aggression discussed negatively by parents or teachers and thereby come to regard it negatively themselves. Operant conditioning of negative evaluations of aggression may occur if children fail to be rewarded or praised for their aggression. As we have already seen, most children do observe at least some models behaving aggressively and receiving rewards of one sort or another as a consequence. At the same time, some of the child's own aggressive behavior may be punished, either directly by parents or indirectly because it failed to achieve its aims. The product of this inconsistency of reward and punishment is apt to be evaluative ambiguity about the usefulness and appropriateness of aggression. The child will be uncertain as to whether aggression is good or bad, justified or not.

Inconsistencies of reward and punishment for aggression and the resulting emotional uncertainty as to its usefulness may make a person hesitant about aggressing and will often result in feelings of guilt or anxiety once aggression has been performed (Averill, 1982). The timing of rewards and punishments is also important in determining the degree of learning. If aggression is punished after a considerable delay (or if it is rewarded immediately), subsequent nonaggressive behavior will be weaker than if the punishment were immediate (or the reward delayed; Walters & Demkow, 1963).

When an individual describes himself as having "lost control," he is saying that he behaved in a way he would prefer not to behave or in a way that he feels does not fit with his view of himself. Why would someone do what he says he prefers not to do? There are at least three reasons. One is to maintain a consistent self-image. If you think of yourself as a nonaggressive person and you have just aggressed, you must either acknowledge that you are not nonaggressive or you must explain the aggression as an aberration, something the "real" you does not do. Second, it may alleviate the aggressor's responsibility for the consequences of his actions. To the extent that the victim can be seen as responsible for "making" the aggressor "lose control," the aggressor cannot be held accountable for what he did not freely do. Third, a person may make statements to himself that justify aggression.

For example, Irene comes home from work an hour late and tells her husband that she had to work for an extra hour. Many husbands would accept this as a reasonable explanation. But if Bill tells himself that being late means he is less important than her boss, then he may feel justified in becoming abusive. Negative self-statements are those that give rise to (and hence justify) negative emotions, such as anger, and actions, such as aggression. Since self-statements that give rise to aggression are learned, changing the things we say to ourselves may also be learned.

A behavior modification program described by Goldstein and Rosenbaum (1982) suggests that becoming upset or angry should be a cue to examine what you are telling yourself. Once these negative self-statements are identified, they should be replaced with positive alternatives. For instance, the negative self-statement, "She knows I hate it when she's late from work," can be replaced by "She knows I don't like it when she's late, so there must be a good reason she isn't home on time. Maybe she was detained at work or by traffic."

Sex Differences in Aggression

The potency of rewards and punishments for learning to inhibit aggression can be seen in the striking sex differences in violent behavior. Males of all ages are more violent than females of comparable ages, and they are arrested for far more crimes (with the exception of vice and prostitution) than females. In 1983, females accounted for 16.6 percent of all arrests. These striking differences are at least partly a result of early training (Adams, 1984).

It is unlikely that sex differences in aggression are primarily the result of biological factors. When other conditions are equal, men and women appear to be equally aggressive. In a national survey of 2,143 American families, 12 percent of the husbands and wives had attacked each other physically in the past year (Straus, Gelles, & Steinmetz, 1979). In half of these families, both spouses attacked each other with equal frequency. In one-fourth, it was the husband who was abusive, and in another fourth it was the wife. In their review of the literature, Frodi, Macaulay, and Thome (1977) report that most studies examining sex differences in aggression fail to find that men are more aggressive than women (see also Hyde, 1984).

We have reviewed evidence suggesting that many criminal offenses are opportunistic (Chapter 3). To the extent that this is so, we would expect that as females gain more opportunities to commit crime, for example, by entering the work force, the crime rates of men and women will converge. This shrinking gap between the rates of male and female offenses has already appeared. Between 1972 and 1981, female arrest rates rose 61 percent, while for men the figure was 51 percent.

Values and Attitudes Toward Violence

A nationwide survey (Blumenthal, Kahn, Andrews, & Head, 1972) found that only about 6 percent of American men regarded all types of violence unfavorably and 3 percent regarded all types of violence favorably. The remaining 91 percent had no unequivocal good or bad label for violence, but instead judged specific acts of violence as good or bad depending upon who was aggressing against whom. Values toward others and their relationship to attitudes toward violence were also studied in the survey. Five types of values were examined: the extent to which an individual believed in retribution; kindness, as embodied in the Golden Rule; the right to self-defense; how people were valued relative to property; and how humanistic values were regarded in comparison to materialistic values.

> Retributiveness and self-defense were most closely related to . . . attitudes (toward violence), while kindness was almost totally unrelated. Not only were the two "pro-violent" values (retributiveness and self-defense) closely related to attitudes about how much force the police should use in the control of disturbances, but there was a high degree of agreement with such values among American men. So it would seem that there are strong values in our country favoring violence for social control, and only weak values that act against it. . . . In summary then, values are related to attitudes toward violence and probably influence such attitudes.

Since the vast majority of people regard violence as neither fully desirable nor fully undesirable, it will be necessary to ex-

amine peoples' own internal standards for deciding whic[
haviors are judged morally right or wrong and in which cir
stances.

Internal Moral Restraints Against Violence

There are at least four kinds of justification that can play a role
in an individual's failure to engage in violent behavior. The first
is because he has no reason, desire, or ability to do so. Second,
even though he may be motivated to aggress, he fails to act violently for fear of punishment, retaliation, or some other force
acting upon him from the external environment; the third is
that, even though motivated to aggress, an individual may have
available a variety of nonaggressive, alternative behaviors which
enable him to cope with provocation nonviolently. Finally, even
though motivated to aggress, an individual may decide *for reasons he provides himself* that it is wrong, immoral, or unwise.
In the last two instances, the individual decides not to aggress
because of internal, rather than external, sources of pressure.

The development of internal moral restraint is a complex and
much-debated issue in contemporary psychology. There are few
definitive studies in this field, and much of what is presented
below is based on current theories of moral development. What
is generally meant by morality is behavior that is internally or
self-regulated; behavior that is judged by the individual against
some internal standard of right or wrong (Wilson, 1973). It
is possible that one's internalized standards are not seen as
"moral" by the community at large. We can imagine a person,
for example, raised and socialized by criminals who internalizes
criminal values, behaviors, and standards. What is characteristic of an internal standard is that it is not dependent on the
sentiments of others once it has developed.

Martin Hoffman (1970) has indicated three types or levels
of behavioral standard. The simplest and most primtive type
involves fear or anxiety. Someone other than the actor must be
present and be potentially capable of rewarding or punishing
the actor's behavior. In the case of aggression, a person operating at this moral level would fail to engage in violence if some

powerful authority figure, such as a parent or a police officer, were present. The individual will not engage in an act because he has been punished for it in the past and may anticipate receiving punishment for engaging in the same act in the future. In the absence of a potentially rewarding or punishing person, there is no reason why the individual should *not* act aggressively. This is not an internal standard, but is based on potential forces from the external environment acting upon the individual. A second type of standard involves the individual's identification with some other person. The individual's actions are based on his views of what the other would approve or disapprove; his behavior is largely designed to be consistent with, and meet the approval of, the other. The person will not act aggressively so long as the individual with whom he identifies is perceived as condemning aggression. In the most advanced type of standard, the individual chooses his actions to meet his own obligations to himself. The individual does not require either the real or symbolic presence of another; he does not aggress because he chooses not to aggress.

How an individual progresses from one behavioral standard to another is a source of debate in psychology (Staub, Bar-Tal, Karylowsky, & Reykowski, 1984). Some have argued that the development of a higher level of moral behavior can be explained wholly or primarily by traditional theories of learning and conditioning (Aronfreed, 1968), while others, most notably Jean Piaget (1937) and Lawrence Kohlberg (1976), have stated that the transition from one level of morality to another is largely because of biological and cognitive maturation. While the processes involved in moral development are controversial, there is general acceptance of the existence of several levels of moral reasoning which people typically display. There are, however, some disagreements between theorists as to what are the levels of morality. Piaget, for example, distinguished between two major moral levels: behavior regulated by a respect for and submission to authority and behavior which is self-regulated. In the former case, an individual obeys rules and laws *because* they are rules and laws which are seen as absolute and immutable. At such a level of moral judgment, the rightness or wrongness of an act is judged on the basis of its consequences; the more damaging an act, the worse it is seen to be, whether it was intentional or accidental. At the higher level of morality, rules and laws are seen as based on cooperative social arrangement and as subject to change. When judging whether an act is right or wrong, the person considers the intentions of the actor rather than simply the consequences of the act. At this level an intentional but slightly damaging act would be seen as more severe than an accidental act resulting in extreme damage.

Kohlberg has refined Piaget's levels of morality to include essentially a six-stage hierarchy. The first stage of moral reasoning involves, as does Piaget's, the avoidance of punishment and deference to authority. At the sixth or highest stage, an individual's behavior is governed by his or her own conscience and by mutual respect and trust.[1]

Important for the transition from one moral level to another is the ability to put oneself in the position of another person, to be able to view behavior from more than a self-interested, egocentric perspective. When one is able to consider another's point of view, one is more likely to consider the other's intentions and feelings. This in turn is likely to result both in greater feelings of sympathy and empathy toward others and in a thought process involving reflection and evaluation which minimizes the tendency toward impulsive action (Staub, 1971). Thus, higher levels of moral judgment are negatively related to aggressiveness. Kohlberg, Scharf, and Hickey (1972) found that adolescent delinquents and adult inmates almost invariably score at the earliest stages of moral reasoning, suggesting that less developed moral reasoning may be a critical factor in delinquency and crime (Edelman & Goldstein, 1981). In other words, the

1. According to Kohlberg (Kohlberg & Turiel, 1971), differences between children of different social classes or cultures are due, not to a difference in values and moral precepts, but to the fact that they progress through the various stages of the hierarchy at different rates.

ability to step outside oneself and view a situation from the viewpoint of another increases self-control, or cognitive control, over one's own behavior and increases the number of behavioral options available. It has also been proposed that conflicts between parties can be reduced more readily by making each state the views of the opposition accurately before discussing those views (Rapoport, 1960). Thus taking another's perspective can not only reduce conflict already present, but can prevent conflict from arising in the first place.

A related factor of importance, which is also compatible with the earlier discussion of impulsivity and delay of gratification in Chapter 2, has been pointed out by Eleanor Maccoby (1968):

> One aspect of cognitive growth which might be related to moral behavior is increasing time span. The young child can neither plan over an extended time nor easily foresee delayed consequences of his actions. Increasing understanding of time sequences should facilitate moral behavior in that it permits more sophisticated understanding of the consequences of actions for oneself and others and permits balancing alternative outcomes in such a way that the individual can forego immediate gratifications for the sake of maximizing long-term gains and minimizing long-term losses. (p. 256)

At higher levels of moral reasoning, then, people are less impulsive and more reflective in their actions, are better able to foresee the consequences of their behavior, are more likely to consider the point of view of the other, and as a consequence, have available to themselves a greater variety of alternative behaviors in which to engage. Closely related to the increase in behavioral alternatives which results from moral development is the intentional fostering of alternative forms of behavior, such as charity and altruism, which can serve as substitute responses to aggression in interpersonal situations.

At the higher levels of moral development it is easier to sympathize with others and such sympathetic emotional responses are generally incompatible with feelings of rage and hostility.

We would therefore expect those operating at higher levels of moral reasoning to engage in behaviors opposite to and incompatible with aggression. To someone operating at an elementary moral level, the sight of a weakling or a drunk on the street may be an invitation to rob or attack, while to someone operating at a higher level of moral judgment, the sight of the same person is apt to elicit positive emotional responses.[2] To the extent that positive emotional responses are present, aggressive behavior is less probable.

Level of moral reasoning is related to a wide variety of behavioral and emotional tendencies. In a number of studies, support has been provided for the notion that higher levels of moral judgment are associated with increased positive social behavior and with decreased antisocial actions. For example, Fishkin, Keniston, and MacKinnon (1973) found the higher levels of Kohlberg's moral reasoning stages to be associated with a rejection of conservative ideology (though it was not related to an acceptance of radical ideology). Individuals at the higher levels of moral reasoning are less likely to engage in cheating than those at lower levels (Kohlberg, 1963). An interesting study by Hudgins and Prentice (1973) compared the level of moral judgment of delinquent and nondelinquent boys and of their mothers. They report that delinquents operated at lower levels of moral reasoning than nondelinquents, and further, that the mothers of delinquents also operated at lower moral judgment levels than the mothers of nondelinquents.

One correlate of increased moral judgment is an increase in the number of alternative behaviors from which an individual can choose in responding to some provocation or threat. Among the most important alternative behaviors are those which are incompatible with aggression, such as charity and altruism.

2. This stands somewhat in contrast to Lerner's notion of the "just world phenomenon" presented in the previous chapter. Berkowitz, 1970, has provided evidence that the just world phenomenon is more likely to be found among those who are uncertain of their own worth, in other words, those with low self-esteem.

The Development of Responses Incompatible
with Aggression

That boys and girls, men and women, differ so greatly in their aggressiveness is due in large measure to the way in which they are reared by their parents or guardians. So it is to child-rearing that we must look first for remedies to the problems of crime and violence.

Those values, attitudes, and behaviors that we characterize as typically masculine tend to promote aggressiveness. After noting the existence of consistent gender differences in aggression, Eron and Huesmann (1984) note:

> We must reexamine what it means to be a man or masculine in our society, since the preponderance of violence in our society is perpetrated by males or by females who are acting like males. It is our contention that if we want to reduce the level of aggression in society, we should also discourage boys from aggression very early in life and reward them for other behaviors. In other words, we should socialize boys more in the manner that we have been socializing girls. Rather than insisting that little girls should be treated like little boys and trained to be aggressive and assertive, it should be the other way around. (pp. 162–163)

We also need to provide children with constructive, nonaggressive ways to resolve and reduce conflict. For very young children, positive forms of social behavior are correlated with aggression. A young child who is aggressive toward another child is also likely to act kindly toward him or her at some other time. Beyond the age of about 6, however, those children who are charitable and helpful toward others show the least amount of aggressive behavior (Murphy, 1937). For older children, and for adults as well, prosocial responses are negatively related to aggression, and to the extent that an individual has learned prosocial behaviors, he or she is not likely to be aggressive. One reason for this relationship is the emotional requirements for prosocial forms of behavior. In order to be charitable and helpful, one must be able to place oneself in the other's position, to see things from the other's point of view. This ability increases sympathy and empathy, making charitableness more likely, and negative, incompatible forms of behavior less likely (Feshbach & Feshbach, 1969).

What tends to make one act prosocially? Hornstein (1973) has suggested three conditions that promote positive social behavior, all involving an increased feeling of commonality with others: aging, the lack of alienation, and an inclusive concept of "we." According to Hornstein's formulation, the more people with whom we feel bonds of community, the more sympathy we feel toward them, and the more apt we are to act prosocially toward them. Aging has the effect of increasing the number of different social groups to which a person belongs, and as the number of groups with which one identifies increases, the number of people toward whom one feels amity increases. Feelings of alienation tend to make the individual feel relatively isolated and powerless and reduce the number of others with whom the person feels common bonds. The obverse of this state, what we might call "individuation" (see Chapter 3), tends to increase feelings of involvement and participation in the social community. If social isolation is a contributing factor in violent crime, as we have suggested in Chapter 3, then integration into a social community can prevent antisocial behavior. Finally, the distinction between one's concept of "we" and "they" is important in determining prosocial behavior. If an individual has an inclusive, broad concept of "we," for example, meaning all humankind, then positive sentiments toward others will be maintained. If other people are seen as outsiders, belonging primarily to groups with which the individual does not identify in any way, there is less reason to sympathize with them and less charity will be extended toward them.

Staub (1975) has suggested a number of additional determinants of prosocial behavior, among the most important of which is the general quality of interaction that occurs between parent and child. To the degree that parents are affectionate and nurturant and to the extent that they use this affection and nurturance to guide and control the child's behavior, the child will develop positive regard for others and an internalized code of moral conduct. Reasoning with the child, pointing out the consequences of his or her actions for others (a process known as *induction*), also increases the child's ability to delay self-interested, egoistic behavior and to consider others' feelings before acting.

Of course, one cannot command parents to love and nurture their children. However, programs have been developed that teach parents to monitor their children's behavior, to reinforce prosocial behavior, and to use nonphysical means of punishment (e.g., Bandura, 1977; Feindler, Marriott, & Iwata, 1984; Patterson, 1982; see Eron & Huesmann, 1984). In general, affectionate, nurturant, inductive parents serve as models of morality for the child. When exposed to prosocial models, children learn and imitate similar responses. It has also been suggested (e.g., Emshoff, Davis, & Davidson, 1981) that prosocial and nonaggressive methods for dealing with conflict be taught in schools. Such a "curriculum" would stress altruistic and sharing behavior using reinforcement, modeling, and role-playing techniques.

Children for whom one or both parents serve as moral models are apt to imitate and eventually to internalize their parents' moral standards. This fact is particularly evident in a study conducted by Perry London and his colleagues (1970). Twenty-seven Christians who rescued Jews from the Nazis in Europe were interviewed in depth about the reasons for their selfless acts. An important finding of the study was that nearly all of the rescuers identified strongly with one of their parents, who served as a highly moral model for their children. An additional finding was that not all of the rescuers acted out of feelings of compassion. One rescuer, a Seventh-Day Adventist minister, was described by London in this way:

Seventh Day Adventists were very marginal socially and not always treated kindly in Holland; his father spent considerable time in jail. Although this minister described himself as mildly anti-Semitic, like his father, during the war he organized a very effective and large-scale operation for rescuing Dutch Jews. The reason he gave for doing so was simply that it was a Christian's duty. (p. 248)

While formal instruction in prosocial behavior and conflict resolution has been called for by many, such skills may also be acquired in everyday activities. Encouraging children to play games that require cooperation, or to work with others in problem-solving activities, are effective ways to increase prosocial behavior and break down barriers between them (Aronson, Blaney, Sikes, Stephan, & Snapp, 1975). In one study, children who participated in cooperative games were more willing to share candy with their classmates (Orlick, 1981).

For adults, as well as children, the availability of nonaggressive responses to conflict reduces reliance on violence. Sports or other engrossing activities may serve as anger-regulating devices, not in the traditional psychoanalytic sense of catharsis, but in the sense of being activities incompatible with aggression. Because humans are the supremely symbolic creatures they are, a remarkable ability exists to transform an emotion, such as a mild insult, into a great wrong by rewriting history or reinterpreting the personal past. For example, a husband who feels slighted by his wife is able to reinterpret events of the past, which had hitherto not been interpreted as rejections, as subtle but intentional attempts to undermine his feelings of worth. A slight anger may thus become a great one, and it is this greater anger that is apt to be acted upon. If a person is sufficiently distracted from the task of revising history the slight anger remains minor and will dissipate with the passage of time. Sports that require coordination and concentration may easily serve this distracting function, thereby preventing a negative emotion from becoming more intense, and may also become associated with the reduction of that emotion. Baron (1983) has found that the

nce of incompatible emotional states, such as humor or
ual arousal, may also reduce the use of aggression.

Situational Nonaggression Factors

Most theorists of moral development regard behavior which is
under one's own regulation—that is, behavior judged by internal
standards—as somehow "more moral" than behavior which is
guided by external standards, such as rules, laws, or coercion. I
have suggested that the reason for this is because external regulation requires the presence—either real or symbolic—of some
potentially rewarding or punishing agent, while self-regulated
behavior does not. Also, internally regulated behavior is likely
to be more consistent across times and situations, while externally regulated behavior will be more unstable, varying with the
circumstances and the particular others present. While it may
be the case that internal regulation is more desirable from the
viewpoint of society than external regulation, it is nevertheless
true that much behavior depends on the specific circumstances
in which the actor finds himself. In this section we consider situ-
ation-specific behaviors.

Situational determinants of aggression were presented in
Chapter 3 where it was proposed that situations account for
at least as much aggressive behavior as the aggressor's personality, early development, and social history. This also seems to
be the case with nonaggressive behavior, particularly prosocial
responses.

While the ideal may be that individuals internalize strong
codes of moral conduct, develop broad and inclusive feelings of
mutuality with others, place themselves in others' positions before deciding which course of action to follow, and follow their
conscience rather than social convention, such an ideal is rarely
realized. The reason for this is because of the inconsistency and
complexity of moral (and legal) codes of conduct as well as
the competing and contradictory features of any given social
situation. For example, while it may be seen as immoral to take

another's life, it seems both legally and morally justifiable to do so if that other person threatens your own life. The difficulty of interpreting actions in complex situations can be seen in the case of the My Lai massacre, which occurred during the Vietnam war. In nationwide surveys conducted in the United States and Australia (Kelman & Lawrence, 1972; Mann, 1973) assessing reactions to the massacre and to the trial of Lt. William Calley, it was found that over half the Americans and nearly one-third of the Australians said that if ordered to shoot civilians, they would follow orders. Thus, there is both a good deal of uncertainty as to which course of action is proper and, for many respondents, some conflict between internal moral codes and external legal codes. Situations are rarely unambiguous, so it becomes necessary to examine the components of situations that give rise to various kinds of definitions and behaviors.

If people generally or frequently fail to operate at some ideal level of morality, what situational factors prevent them from wrong-doing and promote acts of a positive social nature? One is the fear of punishment. Children often refrain from aggressive and other antisocial acts when their parents (or other adults) are present, but engage in them freely when adults are absent. Adults, too, will frequently resist the temptation to transgress when their behavior is, or may be, under surveillance. Probably more important than the fear of direct punishment from others is self-elicited anxiety or guilt which may be aroused by a moral transgression. If, in the past, an individual has been punished or chastised for engaging in some behavior, say, aggression, he may refrain from aggressing even in the absence of others because he may anticipate some punishment (even though there is no one available to punish him) should he aggress. Such anticipation of punishment is roughly equivalent to the concept of anxiety; it is an unpleasant emotional state that is objectively unwarranted by the situation. This anticipation of punishment, or anxiety, may be prevented by not engaging in the aggressive act, thereby avoiding the feeling, or if aggression has already occurred, anxiety may be reduced by self-punishment and self-criticism or by seeking punishment from others (Aronfreed,

1964). Each year many people confess to the police for crimes they did not commit. One explanation for this phenomenon is that they are seeking punishment for some real or imagined transgression which they did commit but for which they failed to receive the anticipated punishment (Bem, 1966; Zimbardo, 1969). Since aggression anxiety is an unpleasant state, we would expect people to try to avoid its occurrence; one way to prevent such anxiety from arising is to avoid engaging in aggressive behavior.

It has been proposed that feelings of alienation tend to reduce prosocial behavior while feelings of individuation increase it. We would thus expect people who live in small towns, as opposed to large cities, to be both more altruistic and less aggressive because of their feelings of integration and visibility in the community. Findings confirming this have been reported in a number of studies (Latané & Darley, 1970).

Newman (1972) suggests that the ability to be seen by others in multi-dwelling housing units acts as a powerful deterrent to crime.

> We find that there are many aspects and facets to surveillance which contribute to the improvement of security. Stated simply, if there is any modicum of morality and accompanying social pressures in a community, opening up all activity in public spaces to natural supervision proves a very powerful deterrent to criminal acts. . . . The subdivision of housing projects into small, recognizable and comprehensible-at-a-glance enclaves is a further contributant to improving the visual surveillance mechanism. Simultaneously, this subdivision serves to provide identity and territorial definition; gives focus, involvement, and commitment to the act of surveillance. In some housing developments, where the surveillance of the activity of one's neighbors, outside their apartments, was possible, residents were found to be very familiar indeed with everyone's comings and goings—and occasionally, somewhat critical. The overall effect, however, was to cement collective identity and responsibility—through these social pressures. (p. 100)

It is of interest here to note the psychological effects that physical structures may have and the resultant influence of these various psychological states. In the examples cited by Newman, particular types of dwelling units enhance feelings of community and identity among residents and, by making any intruder easily identifiable, minimize crime.

Not only does the physical environment influence feelings of identity and behavior, it can also influence the creation of a wide variety of mood states and opportunities for engaging in various acts. Individuals' immediate moods, experiences, and opportunities may influence their prosocial as well as their antisocial tendencies. For example, during the Christmas season opportunities to engage in prosocial behavior are abundant: there are Salvation Army kettles on street corners and in shopping centers, mail-order campaigns for Christmas seals, drives to raise funds, and clothing, food, and toy collections for the needy. The increased number of opportunities for helping are likely to have an "unfreezing" effect on charitable motives; and either by observing the charity of others, who serve as altruistic models (Bryan & Test, 1967), or by experiencing the generally positive emotions that accompany a holiday season (Isen, 1970; Isen & Levin, 1972), individuals are more likely to engage in prosocial behavior themselves. Positive opportunities and emotional states facilitate prosocial behavior and impede aggression.

In the same way that a single act of aggression may promote subsequent aggressive acts, so too may a single act of charity facilitate subsequent altruistic acts by the same person. For example, Freedman and Fraser (1966) made a simple, small request of people and later made a larger request of them. Those who complied with the first request were more likely to comply with the second. By the same token, once one has engaged in prosocial behavior, there may be an increased tendency to continue to act positively toward others.

The aggression model used throughout this book may be modified slightly to account for this effect and to generate expectations about other aspects of altruistic behavior. Once there is some incentive to engage in prosocial behavior (for example, hearing a cry for help), an individual will evaluate the situation in order to determine whether that prosocial incentive is stronger than the competing elements in the setting which call for a non-helping response (for example, the potential danger involved, the loss of time and energy). If the prohelping factors are seen to outweigh the nonhelping factors, then the individual will offer assistance. Once such action has occurred, the individual will justify his or her behavior by reevaluating the situation and the individuals involved. It is this reevaluation, which amounts to a cognitive justification for helping, that facilitates helping on subsequent occasions. In a study (Goldstein, Davis, & Herman, 1975) reported in Chapter 3, it was shown that once an individual acted prosocially toward another he or she subsequently engaged in increasing amounts of prosocial behavior as the experiment progressed.

There is generally a conflict involved in helping another person, either because of the costs of time, energy, money, and potential danger involved or cultural norms that stress minding one's own business. This conflict is resolved in much the same way that aggression conflict is resolved: the individual attempts to make sense out of the situation by weighing each of its component elements. When the prohelping factors are seen to outweigh the nonhelping factors, help will ensue. The weighting of the people, settings, and behaviors involved depends both on long-term factors, such as exposure to helping models and rewards for helping in the past, and on situational factors, such as the estimated costs and rewards for helping in that particular situation. As with aggression, once a helping act has occurred, it will tend to be justified by the individual's reevaluating more positively the prohelping elements and devaluing the nonhelping elements.

Before going on to discuss the control of violence, it might serve us well to summarize the contributing factors to aggression which have been presented so far. Table 4.2 contains a listing of the causative aggression and nonaggression factors reviewed in Chapters 2 through 4.

TABLE 4.2   Factors Associated with Aggression and Nonaggression

Short-term	Long-term
Aggression	
Characteristics of the actor:	*Characteristics of the actor:*
Immediately prior aggressive acts.	Deindividuation.
Loss of cognitive control of behavior.	Impulsivity.
Low identifiability.	Low level of moral judgment.
Moderate amount of alcohol ingestion.	Negative labels for targets.
Moderate emotional arousal.	Positive labels for aggression.
Consequences of actor's behavior:	*Consequences of actor's behavior:*
Cognitive justification for aggression.	Rewards for aggression.
Devaluation of victim.	*Parental characteristics:*
Environmental factors:	Aggressive models, unpunished.
Abundant opportunities for aggression.	High punitiveness.
Availability of a weapon.	*Environmental factors:*
Familiar environment.	Aggressible situations.
Familiar or similar target.	Exposure to aggression in others.
Recent exposure to violence.	
Nonaggression	
Characteristics of the actor:	*Characteristics of the actor:*
Aggression anxiety, guilt.	Ability to delay gratification.
Arousal of pleasant emotions.	Ability to take role of others.
Fear of punishment.	High level of moral judgment.
High identifiability.	Inclusive concept of "we."
Immediately prior nonagressive acts.	Individuation.
Environmental factors:	Negative labels for aggression.
Presence of authority figure (for those low in moral judgment).	Positive regard for others.
Unfamiliar environment.	*Consequences of actor's behavior:*
	Rewards for nonaggression.
	Parental characteristics:
	Affection, control, nurturance.
	Nonaggressive models.
	Environmental factors:
	Nonaggressible situations.

Note: The characteristics of the actor listed under short-term factors are temporary or transient states, most often induced by the physical or social environment, rather than enduring traits of the actor.

5
Reduction and Control of Aggression

Psychologists and sociologists have been studying aggression and crime for decades. They do not know a great deal about the causes of these devastating problems, yet our relative state of ignorance should not prevent us from doing what we can in the service of a more peaceful and just society. What Karl Menninger wrote in 1968 is apt today: ". . . we have at hand great quantities of research findings which clearly indicate what we should be doing. Much indeed we don't know, but we are not doing one-tenth of what we should about what we already do know." In this and the following chapter we discuss what we might do based on what we already know.

There are two strategies for controlling violence and crime. The first involves short-term solutions that would increase the costs or reduce the opportunities for committing aggressive and criminal acts. This approach does not alter the actor's motivation to commit mayhem—it merely makes it less convenient for him to do so. The second approach relies not on surveillance and reduced opportunity but on a reduced motivation to commit antisocial acts.

The theoretical model that we have been using states that aggressive behavior is the result of four factors: long-term and situational factors that are associated positively, and those that are associated negatively, with aggression. The likelihood of aggressive behavior is determined by the ratio of these two sets of competing tendencies. The model implies that aggression can be lessened in at least four ways: by reducing long-term and/or situational pro-aggression factors, and by increasing long-term and/or situational nonaggression factors. Long-term factors, characterized as internalized aspects of an individual's personality that arise during socialization, are discussed in Chapter 6. Situational factors, characterized as more or less ephemeral, short-lived, and external to the individual's personality, are discussed in this chapter.

Is Crime a Psychological Problem?

It has been assumed throughout this book that the problems of crime and violence are primarily psychological. After all, they are behaviors that involve the interaction of two or more individuals, and this is the primary concern of social psychology. Yet these problems are not *merely* psychological. Rather, as complex behaviors they have political, social, psychological, and economic components, and one can look at violence and crime from any of these perspectives. For example, Henry and Short (1954) and Hovland and Sears (1940) have found economic correlates of homicide and suicide, while Feierabend and Feierabend (1966) have explored the economic and political conditions conducive to large-scale violence. Yet even economic bases of behavior may ultimately depend upon psychological variables, such as people's perceptions of their relative economic well-being, or their abilities to cope with stressful events.

Stress, whether it arises from internal sources such as anxiety, or from economic conditions such as unemployment and inflation, is associated with aggressive behavior (Landau, 1984;

Landau & Beit-Hallahmi, 1983; Messner, 1980). In a study conducted in the Netherlands and the United States, Huppes (1976) focused on inflation as a social stressor. The rate of inflation was positively correlated with violent crime, property crime, suicide, homicide, and divorce.[1]

The relationship between stress and violence is not unidirectional. Individual and societal stress increase violence and crime, but violence and crime also contribute to people's experience of stress (Cohn, Kidder, & Harvey, 1978). The general level of violence in a society influences even automobile accidents. A study by Sivak (1983) found that within the 50 states, the homicide rate successfully predicts the traffic fatality rate. Violence also influences the individual's level of stress as manifest in the fear of crime.

Despite political and economic efforts to control violence, without social support such efforts are bound to fail. As the National Commission on the Causes and Prevention of Violence (1968) has noted:

> For remedial social change to be an effective moderator of violence, the changes must command a wide measure of support throughout the community. Official efforts to impose change that is resisted by a dominant majority frequently prompts counter-violence.

In discussing solutions to the problems of violent crime it will often be necessary to go beyond the psychological bases discussed earlier. While the solutions to violence are seen as largely psychological—that is, as requiring changes in the learning of values, behaviors, and norms—it will be necessary to implement them politically and to develop widespread social and economic support for them.

Like other branches of science, psychology does not have sufficient justification for suggesting social policy. Therefore, in offering remedies, it will be necessary to go beyond existing the-

---

1. This relationship does not hold for every country, however. The correlation between inflation and homicide in Japan is negative (Landau, 1984).

ory and research. The proposals that follow should be thought of as hypotheses that need to be tested on a small scale before they are considered as policy (Campbell, 1969). Some of these solutions may work and others may not, but it is important that whatever solutions to social problems are ultimately implemented they not contradict what we know about those problems from a scientific standpoint (Varela, 1970).

Short-Term Remedial Strategies

The Physical Environment and Crime Control

The character played by Woody Allen in his film *Take the Money and Run,* upon being asked why he was a thief, remarked that it's an occupation in which you can set your own hours, meet interesting people, be your own boss, have an opportunity to travel, and receive excellent wages. There is some truth in this assessment. When the environment presents few obstacles, crime becomes a temptation that to many is irresistible. The easier it is to commit a crime, the more individuals will be seduced into doing it.

If, as I have argued, most crimes and acts of violence are committed by not atypical people who are momentarily instigated and who have an appropriate target and means of aggressing, then the environment can be altered to minimize the opportunity and means to aggress or violate the law, maximize cognitive control over behavior, decrease the tendency for impulsive action, and heighten the actor's feelings of identifiability. The environment can be restructured to reduce the opportunity, attractiveness, and rewards for antisocial behavior.

To take a simple example, research has been conducted on means to reduce the illegal use of slugs in parking meters. Decker (1972) reports research in which structural features of parking meters were altered to minimize slug use. In New York City in 1970, over 3 percent of all parking meter insertions were slugs. Had money been inserted instead of slugs, the total in additional revenues to the city would have been in the neighborhood of a half-million dollars. Two studies were conducted in an effort to determine the most effective means of reducing slug use. In one study, three different regions of the city were chosen, and in each region a different label was attached to each parking meter. The labels read:

> *Slug use is a violation of New York City Ordinance: $50 fine.*
>
> *Slug use is a violation of state law: 3 months imprisonment and $500 fine.*
>
> *Slug use is a federal crime: 1 year imprisonment and $1,000 fine.*

A fourth region was considered a control region and no labels were attached to the meters.

In a second study, Duncan VIP meters were installed in selected experimental regions. The Duncan parking meter rejects many types of slug and also displays the most recently inserted coin in a coin-view window. Thus, in the first study variations in the potential punishment for slug use were introduced, while in the second study, physical characteristics of parking meters were altered.

Decker reports that the use of slugs declined in all of the areas in which labels were used, as well as in the control area in which no label was used. There were no significant differences in the rate of decline among the four areas studied. Hence, the use of the various warning labels was considered to have no effect since there was as much decline in slug usage in the no label (control) region as in the other three regions. However, in the areas in which the new Duncan meters were installed, declines in the rate of slug use were dramatic. Compared with the same areas before the installation of the new meters, slug usage declined from 26 percent in one region to 80 percent in another. Decker concludes:

> It is obvious that the parking meters with the coin-view window and slug-rejector device were more effective in reducing

illicit slug use than use of warning labels. The minimal deterrent value of the labels can probably be attributed to the slim chance a slug user will be apprehended, much less convicted and subjected to the maximum penalty. This might indicate that potential slug users are not greatly deterred by the coin-view window either, since the object of the window is also to instill fear of apprehension. Hence, it seems that a mechanical device, such as the slug-rejector, which makes law violation difficult, is superior to a scheme or device which is dependent upon the potential violator's fear of apprehension. This finding is critical in light of the theoretical structure of criminology based on a punishment-deterrence-rehabilitation model, and it suggests a serious look at programs based on a prevention model and environmental design. (p. 142)

While the Decker report raises the interesting possibility that crime can be deterred by particular environmental features, the question arises as to whether more serious crimes can be so deterred. Although only limited research has been conducted on the effects of environmental modification, what little there is suggests that intelligent and well-planned changes in architectural and urban design can bring about a reduction of violent crime and theft.

Oscar Newman (1972) discusses the case of Clason Point Gardens, a two-story public housing development in the Bronx, New York, consisting of 400 duplex apartments located in over 40 row-house buildings. Elderly white families comprise 33 percent of the tenants, Puerto Rican families 25 percent, and black families about 30 percent. Newman states:

Preliminary interviews revealed that tenants were extremely fearful of being victimized by criminals, both during the day and in the evening; they had severely changed or curtailed their patterns of activity as a result of the atmosphere of heightened danger; they felt they had no right to question, and were afraid to question, the presence of strangers as a means of anticipating and preventing crimes before they occurred. Adolescents from neighboring projects used the grounds as a congregation area, instilling fear and anger in many Clason Point residents. (pp. 165–166)

Newman conducted interviews with the residents of the project in order to clarify what types of design changes were needed, and reasoned that increased tenant surveillance of the grounds, greater definition of the functions of the grounds, an increased sense of propriety by the residents, and a reduction of intergenerational conflict among residents were required. A variety of design changes was made in the project including the following:

> To highlight the public quality of the major pedestrian walk, the design called for (1) widening of the path, using colored and decoratively scored paving; (2) differentiating small private areas (front lawns) outside each dwelling from the public path with low, symbolic walls; and (3) the addition of public seating in the center of the public path, located at a distance from private dwellings sufficient to eliminate conflicts over use, but close enough to be under constant surveillance by residents. At selected intersections of the primary and secondary paths, "play-nodes" were to be created for young children—with seating nearby to allow for supervision. New and decorative lighting was to be employed to highlight the new public paths and recreation areas at night, so as to extend the residents' surveillance potential and feeling of security. (pp. 167–169)

In addition, buildings were refaced in a variety of colors selected by the tenants. The one area of Clason Point which residents felt was most dangerous was the central green space. This area was transformed into special use areas for young children, teenagers, and adults (see Figures 5.1 and 5.2). Newman hoped to turn the central area from a desolate one into the "new focus of Clason Point."

The results of the transformation of Clason Point are summarized by Newman:

> At this writing the rehabilitation of the project has been complete for over twelve months. During this test period, felonies were down to one-third of the previous year's level. Measures

Figure 5.1 View of Central Square before modifications. The most dangerous area in Clason Point Gardens was identified both through tenant interviews and police reports as being the central square. This photo shows the square as it was, including a few benches and one pair of centrally located lights. (Photo by O. Newman. Reprinted with permission.)

of tenant satisfaction showed statistically significant improvement in the reduction of fear, in increased surveillance on the part of tenants, and in their evaluation of the quality of their living environment. The newly modified central play area is very intensively used by the community, and this has succeeded in discouraging its use by drunks and addicts. Tenants now maintain some 80 percent of the project grounds, appreciably reducing the workload of the maintenance staff. (p. 174)

Figure 5.2 View of modified central area. The area has been transformed into a community recreation facility. It has been extensively lighted for night use. (Photo by O. Newman. Reprinted with permission.)

The psychological effects of various features of architectural design and spatial charcteristics of the environment are only in the initial stages of exploration (e.g., Ittelson & Proshansky, 1972). Nevertheless, conditions that increase the individual's sense of self, that is, those that maximize identifiability by others and the possibility of discovery and apprehension, will diminish the tendency to engage in antisocial acts. The design changes reported by Newman increased both the use of formerly unused areas and the visibility of open spaces. These in turn discouraged trespassers and loiterers and led to a reduction in the rate of crime, most probably by increasing would-be offenders' reflection on the consequences of such acts.

Newman also discusses the attempts of the upper- and middle-class urban resident to maximize safety by moving to high-rise luxury apartments protected by electronic surveillance systems and round-the-clock doormen. Tenants are likely to have double-locked doors, a wide-angle viewer in entrance doors, and other security devices. While such measures of safety may add to the immediate security of the urban unpoor, they present dangers to the community on a larger scale.

> When people begin to protect themselves as individuals and not as a community, the battle against crime is effectively lost. The indifferent crowd witnessing a violent crime is by now an American cliché. The move of middle- and upper-class populations into protective high-rises and other structures of isolation—as well guarded and as carefully differentiated from the surrounding human landscape as a military post—is just as clearly a retreat into indifference. The form of buildings and their arrangement can either discourage or encourage people to take an active part in policing while they go about their daily business. "Policing" is not intended to evoke a paranoid vision but refers to the oldest concept in the Western political tradition: the responsibility of each citizen to ensure the functioning of the *polis*. (Newman, 1972, p. 15)

A particular danger of the middle- and upper-class enclave in the city is that it provides security by limiting access to the building. "This usually means walling off a 2- to 10-acre housing complex from the surrounding neighborhood. By this action, thousands of feet of street are removed from all forms of social and visual contact. A natural mechanism providing safety to our streets has been sacrificed to insure the security of the residents of the walled-off complex."

There are alternatives to the high-rise enclaves in which mutual surveillance of the streets and the buildings would be achieved. By maximizing the use of glass in lobbies, corridors, and apartments and by increasing the number of entrances, the streets could be easily observed by the residents of the complex and the complex by those in the street. The building would thus be an integrated and integral part of the community rather than isolated from it.

Aside from arranging buildings in such a way as to increase surveillance by occupants and passersby, it is possible to minimize opportunities for crime by altering other characteristics of the environment. For example, nearly half the automobiles stolen each year have had the keys left in them by their owners. Removing the keys reduces the opportunity (or makes it more difficult) to steal the car. In 1965, when Chevrolet eliminated the "off" position from the ignition system—which previously enabled one to start the car without a key—thefts of Chevrolets dropped 50 percent from the previous year (President's Commission on Law Enforcement and Administration of Justice, 1968).

While such "environmental" measures may reduce criminal activity, it is unclear whether their effects are long-lasting. When American automobile manufacturers began to install devices that would lead to the use of sealt belts, such as a noxious buzzer that could be terminated only by fastening one's seat belt, it was not long before motorists figured out ways to "fool" the safety device; many drivers left the belts permanently fastened behind them or disconnected the buzzer. Devices designed to prevent theft and burglary may lead to more ingenious methods among those who are determined to steal. Nevertheless, many crimes are crimes of opportunity, and if opportunities are reduced, such as through increased street lighting and better door latches, crimes which otherwise would be committed will not be.

One measure that would save thousands of lives anually, and which may indirectly be linked with aggression, would be the installation of a device that would prevent cars from being started by drunk drivers. The device would consist of either a "breathalyzer" to determine the extent of alcohol in the driver's system or a reaction-time device which an inebriated driver could not operate satisfactorily.

Weapons as Aggression-Instigating Objects

In 1980, handguns killed 11,522 Americans. Compare this figure with those for handgun deaths in other countries:

Australia	4
Britain	8
Canada	8
Sweden	18
Israel	23
Switzerland	24
Japan	77

The homicide rate of the United States is from 2 to 70 times the rate for Australia, Austria, Canada, Denmark, England and Wales, Finland, France, Greece, Hong Kong, Hungary, Ireland, Israel, Italy, Japan, the Netherlands, New Zealand, Poland, Scotland, Spain, Sweden, Switzerland, and West Germany. One of the most perplexing problems facing any student of violence is why Americans seem so violent when compared to others with whom they otherwise have so much in common.[2]

A number of explanations have been offered for this disproportionate violence (e.g., Campbell, 1970; Pinkney, 1972; Shure, 1969, 1984). It has been suggested that our history has been a violent one, that a nation born of revolution has a tradition of violence. It has also been proposed that the omnipresence of violence in the mass media is responsible for the high rate of interpersonal aggression reflected in our homicide statistics. Our particular brand of capitalism, in which competition in the economic sphere generalizes to competition in all

2. Before conclusions are drawn from these figures alone, it should be pointed out that different countries, and even localities within countries, have different procedures for defining and recording crime, and that a number of countries have higher homicide rates than the United States (for example, Sri Lanka, Colombia, Kuwait, Taiwan, and Venezuela).

areas of social conduct, has been seen as the basis of violence in the society. The permissiveness of the society has also been held responsible, both with respect to our child-rearing practices and our system of jurisprudence—parents who are permissive with their children and courts that are lenient toward criminals have been seen as the causes of American violence.

While there may be some justification for each of these claims, a more realistic picture incorporates all of them, as well as other features of American life. Violence is, to use a phrase popular in social science, "overdetermined." That is, there is no one cause of even a single act of violence, but rather a series of events and antecedents that contribute to the crime and to the crime rate. Of those countries with much lower violent crime rates than the United States, some were also born of revolution, some also have a relatively high incidence of violence in their popular media, some also have capitalist economies, and some are more lenient in child-rearing and their attitudes toward criminals. One feature that may partially account for the differences in violent deaths is the relative unavailability of lethal weapons, particularly handguns, in most other industrialized nations. Because of the abundance of firearms in the United States, the opportunity to commit homicide is considerably greater than in most other countries.

Since the turn of the century, over three-quarters of a million citizens have been killed by gunfire in the United States. Each year, over 20,000 Americans are shot to death and over 200,000 are seriously injured by firearms. There is nearly one rifle, shotgun, or handgun for every two citizens of this country. In Britain, there are fewer than 1 million licensed rifles, handguns, and shotguns among all its 55 million inhabitants.

While there is some evidence that the mere possession or presence of a lethal weapon leads to increased violence, this evidence is in dispute (see Chapter 3). A more conservative statement would be that, when an individual is bent on aggression in the first place, the presence of a weapon will eventuate in its use, and the consequence of the aggressive act will be much more severe than if no weapon were available. An angry husband may yell at his wife and may even hit her; if a knife is handy, he is more likely to stab her, and there is about a 1 in 30 chance that she will die of the stabbing. If a gun is handy, she is likely to be shot and will die in close to one-sixth of such shooting incidents. The nearly 100 million firearms in this country undoubtedly contribute to the American homicide rate, either directly by serving to provoke aggression or indirectly by enlarging the consequences and seriousness of aggression.

Morris and Hawkins (1970) make several recommendations concerning gun control:

> All firearms—handguns, rifles, and shotguns—must be registered and all persons required to obtain a license to possess or carry any such weapon. . . . Other than in exceptional cases, a license to possess a handgun will be restricted to the police and to authorized security agencies. . . . Gun clubs, hunting clubs, and similar sporting associations using firearms will be required to store the firearms used by their members on club premises and to maintain close security over them (pp. 63–67)

However, such solutions to this problem are made complex largely because of opposition expressed by a number of individuals and groups with vested interests in maintaining the current system of manufacture and distribution of lethal weapons.

Morris and Hawkins go on to consider the traditionally posed objections to their gun-control proposals. They refute the notion that, if guns were not available, murderers would simply use other weapons. Guns are more fatal than other weapons and therefore cause more deaths. It is also argued by some that when guns are outlawed a substantial illegal weapons trade will arise. But murderers are often relatively average people with no long history of previous violence; the availability of guns makes them murderers instead of simple assaulters.

It is further recommended that all ammunition for firearms and all firearms themselves be made with radioactive tracer elements in them so that the presence of such weapons can be detected electronically. Morris and Hawkins also suggest that means for voluntary surrender of firearms without threat of penalty be provided and that the government offer to buy guns back at higher than traditional rates to minimize the temptation to sell guns on the black market. Such steps as restrictive licensing and the surrender of firearms may diminish considerably the rate of death due to homicide, suicide, and accident, but unless additional measures are provided for disarming the American people, there will still be a significant number of preventable, premature deaths in this country because of firearms. Morris and Hawkins recommend severe penalties for weapons offenses and the banning of all sales of weapons through the mail. Such measures will indeed reduce the number of firearms in private hands, but a long-term goal is to make weapons unavailable to those who could use them lethally. It is proposed here that the manufacture of firearms be phased out and that their production ultimately be prohibited except under contract to an official agency of government. If citizens are disarmed sufficiently, then the often legitimate assumption of law-enforcement officials that those suspected of crimes should be considered "armed and dangerous" will no longer be warranted, and the final step in disarmament will be a prohibition against carrying weapons by the police, along the lines of the British system, in which each police precinct has a few expert marksmen who are used in situations in which the police are fired upon. Insofar as the Constitutional issue of disarmament is concerned, Morris and Hawkins state: "We are confident this [disarmament] offends no Constitutional sanctity; we do not oppose a militia whose right to bear arms is guaranteed by the Constitution."

Crime and Time and Punishment

Crime and Sentencing

One factor discussed as a situational determinant of nonaggression is fear of punishment. If an individual anticipates punishment he or she is less likely to engage in aggressive behavior (Dengerink, 1971; Knott, Lasater, & Shuman, 1974). The larger question concerns the circumstances under which fear of punishment will be aroused. It is frequently suggested that penalties, ranging from monetary fines to probation to imprisonment, serve as deterrents to crime by arousing fear or anxiety in the would-be criminal.

When violence occurs in the presence of others, both the actor and the observer show increased aggressiveness (Felson, Ribner, & Siegel, 1984). Of course, we know from social-learning theory that publicity given to violence also enhances aggressiveness among vicarious observers. These effects, as indicated in Chapter 2, are curtailed when the aggressor receives immediate punishment for his aggression. In the instance of criminal violence, punishment for aggression, if it is forthcoming at all, is usually delayed by lengthy legal proceedings. Hence, those who read about violence in their newspapers or see it on television news are essentially observers of unpunished aggressive models. Surveys of crime and subsequent legal proceedings indicate that only a minority of those suspected of engaging in criminal violence are apprehended. (See Table 5.1.) In fact, based on victimization surveys we know that many violent crimes go unreported to the police, particularly cases of rape and family violence. Of those who are apprehended for a

TABLE 5.1   Reported Crimes Cleared by Arrest, 1981

Murder	72%
Aggravated assault	58
Rape	48
Robbery	24
Larceny-theft	19
Burglary	14
Motor vehicle theft	14
All FBI Index Crimes	19%

Source: U.S. Department of Justice, Bureau of Justice Statistics, "Report to the Nation on Crime and Justice," 1983, p. 52.

TABLE 5.2   Median Prison Sentence (in years) by Type of Offense

Offense	Median Sentence	
	Minimum	Maximum
All crimes	4.3	8.6
Violent	5.6	13.3
Murder/attempted murder	10.5	21.9
Rape	5.8	14.9
Robbery	5.4	12.8
Property	2.7	5.6
Burglary	2.9	5.7
Larceny/auto theft	2.4	5.2
Forgery/fraud	2.6	5.4
Drug	3.0	5.7

Source: U.S. Department of Justice, Bureau of Justice Statistics, "Report to the Nation on Crime and Justice," 1983, adapted from p. 76.

crime, there is usually a considerable delay in bringing them to trial, so that if punishment is delivered to the aggressor, it is long after the aggressive act has occurred. In most cases of criminal violence, punishment is either nominal or not delivered at all (see Table 5.2).

After being arrested for a violent crime, a defendant may be called before a judge where well over half of those arrested for serious personal crimes will be released on bail. The defendant is apt to be "on good behavior" between the time he is apprehended and the time his case is heard in court, since any further misconduct is likely to result in a more severe sentence. The period between arrest and disposition of a case often exceeds one year, during which time most defendants lead noncriminal lives. The case, after this lengthy delay, now comes to trial and, assuming the defendant is found guilty and the judge is so disposed, the defendant is sentenced to some term in prison. Psychologically, what effects will this sequence of events have?

First, we can ask what effects the punishment (prison sentence) is supposed to have, and second, what effects it may actually have.

Prison sentences are designed to serve several functions, although legal experts disagree on the relative importance of these: a *retributive* function, designed to punish the criminal for his misdeed; a *rehabilitative* function, designed to minimize the likelihood that the act will be repeated by the criminal in the future; a *deterrent or communicative* function, designed to serve as a warning to others that the act will be dealt with severely should they engage in it; a *protective* function, designed to segregate the criminal from the rest of society. One function often overlooked in such discussions is that criminal sentences are designed to make individuals accept *responsibility* for their actions.

According to one of the most well-established principles in psychology, the "law of effect," we know that events closest in time to a punishment are more severely retarded by the punishment than events further removed from the punishment. In the typical case that we have described, an aggressive act occurs at $Time_1$ followed by nonaggressive acts at $Time_2$ followed by punishment at $Time_3$. According to the law of effect, behavior closest in time to the punishment will be more influenced by the punishment than behavior farther removed from it. Thus, the punishment is likely to have a greater effect on $Time_2$ behavior, the nonaggressive acts, than on $Time_1$ behavior, the aggressive act. Of course, the defendant knows that the punishment is being administered to him because of his aggression and not because of the behavior intervening between that act and the punishment, and so the punishment will probably have at least some impact on the future likelihood of the particular aggressive act. Nevertheless, the longer the delay between aggression and its punishment, the less effective the punishment in retarding aggressive behavior. The typically long delay in our present system may severely retard whatever rehabilitative effect the punishment might otherwise have.

With respect to observers or those who learn of the crime and its subsequent punishment, we can ask what psychological principles might be invoked to explain the effects of punishment as a deterrent or communicative device. Given the long delay between a criminal act of violence and its subsequent disposition by the courts, two processes are relevant. First is the probability that the act itself will be punished, rewarded, or neither. We saw in Chapter 2 that only when aggressive acts were punished was an observer unlikely to learn and imitate the aggressive behavior of the actor in appropriate circumstances. In the vast majority of cases an aggressive act occurs which observers see going unpunished (Barlett & Steele, 1973; Campbell, 1970).

In many of these cases, as well as in some of the instances in which punishment is imposed, the publicity given to the defendant may serve as a positive reinforcement to observers. That is, observers may perceive having one's name in the newspaper or mentioned on television as a reward, and this may increase the chances that observers will imitate the aggression. Former Attorney General Ramsey Clark (1970) has noted:

> People otherwise docile for the time respond to reports of violence as if it were a contagious disease and the reports were a carrier. And for the kid from the slums the only time he is likely to see his picture in the paper may be when he is in police custody following arrest for a violent crime. Far from destroying a reputation, this is the best chance for fame— or at least notoriety—that fate offers him. (p. 33)

To most observers at least some aspects of crime are rewarding, and since punishment to the aggressor occurs in only a minority of cases, the criminal justice system in the United States can have only minimal deterrent effect. If this is unconvincing, add to it the period of months and often years that intervene between crime and punishment. After such a long period of time observers will probably dissociate the punishment from the crime. Not only does the long delay minimize the effectiveness of punishment on the aggressor, it also minimizes its effectiveness as a communication to observers.[3]

One purpose of imprisonment is to protect society from the criminal by removing him for a time from the community. Well over 90 percent of all prisoners, however, are ultimately released from prison to rejoin the community. While in prison the convict will associate with those who are more versed in violence than himself, may be subjected to inhumane conditions and degrading treatment, and is apt to leave prison a greater threat to society than when he first entered. Coupled with the label of "criminal" or "ex-convict," a former prisoner is often unable to find suitable employment and, being considered a social deviant by those in the community, will often have among his associates other social deviants. These are the very circumstances optimal for the commission of further crimes. So while imprisonment may temporarily protect society (an arguable point), in the long run society is worse off for having imprisoned the offender. If social isolation contributes to violent crime, as we have argued in Chapter 2, then continued removal of offenders from mainstream society can only enhance subsequent violence. Furthermore, since prisons are a part of society, the violence that occurs within them should figure into the tabulations of violence in the society as a whole; prisons merely serve to displace the violence—but only temporarily—from "us" to "them."

Prison sentences are also designed to function as sheer punishment or retribution, independent of their deterrent, protective, or rehabilitative effects. Whether or not this is a proper function of prison is a moral, and perhaps a Constitutional, issue beyond the scope of this book; from a psychological perspective, the imposition of punishment for retributive purposes is highly interwoven with its other stated functions. By being

3. There are studies of legal sanctions and crime, most of which show a negligible correlation between the two (Bailey & Smith, 1972; Chambliss, 1966; Sellin, 1967; Tittle, 1969; Van Den Haag & Conrad, 1983).

retributive and punitive, society encourages retribution and punishment by the population as a whole.

Finally, prison sentences, as well as other forms of punishment, are designed to make individuals accept responsibility for their behavior. This function is well served by penalties for criminal conduct. Even though I have argued that much violence is instigated by situational factors, such as opportunity and other features of the physical and social environment, it is nonetheless true that people exercise a choice in placing themselves in certain situations. Exposure to opportunity may facilitate crime, but to the extent that people place themselves in situations where opportunity is maximized, they are morally responsible for their behavior (even if the behavior would also have been engaged in by other individuals in similar circumstances). Every individual's actions are a product of his times, but the times cannot be held accountable for the actions of the individual. While criminal sanctions do hold individuals responsible for their actions, the law recognizes that occasionally environmental pressures exerted on an actor are so potent that the actor should not be held accountable for his behavior. Two legally acceptable means of absolving an aggressor of responsibility are the "temporary insanity" plea and the self-defense, or justifiable homicide, defense.

Capital Punishment

During crime waves and political election campaigns there are increased calls for the death penalty. Of the industrialized nations of the world, only the United States, Japan, South Africa, and the Soviet Union have capital punishment.

The death penalty is presumed to be a deterrent to crime. Research on the deterrent effects of capital punishment not only fails to demonstrate a subsequent decline in crime following an execution (Brier & Fienberg, 1980; Lofton, 1980; cf. Ehrlich, 1975), but sometimes has found an imitative effect, with homicide rates increasing after an execution (Bowers & Pierce, 1980).

If capital punishment is a more effective deterrent than long imprisonment, its abolition ought to be followed by homicide rate increases. In a cross-cultural study of 14 nations that abolished the death penalty, Archer and Gartner (1984a) found that abolition was followed more often than not (in 57 percent of the countries) by absolute *decreases* in homicide rates, not by the increases (which occurred in only 5 of the 14 countries) predicted by deterrence theory. They conclude that:

> while there may be many persuasive reasons for capital punishment—including arguments based on retribution, economics, or other principles—the deterrence of potential offenders cannot be included among them. Other justifications for the death penalty can and presumably will be debated, but the deterrence hypothesis must be regarded at this time as scientifically unsupported. (p. 137)

Our discussion of crime and sentencing suggests that punishment fails to serve at least three of its primary functions—rehabilitation, protection, and deterrence. Much of this failure can be blamed on the long delay in bringing cases to a conclusion, but much of it resides as well in the nature of imprisonment. Punishment, if it is to reduce criminal violence, must follow as soon as possible the act it is designed to alter and must also refrain from influencing the offender's values, attitudes, and behavior to the long-term detriment of society.

Reducing Crimes: Decriminalization

If we examine the role of the police as potential deterrents to crime, we immediately become entangled in a complex network of police duties, functions, attitudes, and values (Klockars, 1985). The police act as traffic regulators, social workers, lawyers, detectives, a lost-and-found, bicycle and taxicab registrars, escorts, enforcers of law, and moral guardians.

Over half of all arrests made by the police in the United States involve what are typically referred to as "victimless crimes," that is, crimes that involve no personal or property damage or loss to anyone other than the offender (drunkenness, vagrancy, sex and narcotics law violations, gambling, and so on).[4] These victimless crimes accounted for over 5 million arrests in 1981, more than twice the number of arrests for "serious crimes," those seven "index crimes" which the FBI considers serious in its Uniform Crime Reports: murder, aggravated assault, rape, robbery, burglary, larceny, and auto theft.

It is questionable whether victimless crimes should occupy police involvement at all, not so much on the grounds that they involve arbitrary standards of morality as on the grounds that they prevent the police from performing other more essential duties and may, in fact, undermine respect for the law and its agents.

The police insist that they are simply enforcing existing laws in prosecuting victimless crimes, but the police do not enforce all laws nor prosecute all suspects equally (Clark, 1970; President's Commission, 1968), which may weaken support for, and cooperation with, the police. For example, the kinds of crime considered serious by the FBI may be perceived as harassment of the poor since crimes committed by the wealthy are not pursued by the police with the same vigor, or are not considered sufficiently serious to warrant prosecution. As Jessica Mitford (1973) notes: "Absent from the Uniform Crime Reports are crimes committed by the rich and powerful against the rest of the population: murder, assault, and theft via violation of health and safety codes by slum landlords, mine owners, construction companies, robbery by the food industry through deceptive packaging, and organized crime that depends on corruption of public officials, to name a few" (p. 64). Also, the types of victimless crimes enforced by the police are those in which minorities and the poor are likely to be overrepresented; if they are not overrepresented among offenders, they are certainly overrepresented among those prosecuted.

---

4. While there is widespread agreement that gambling, sex, and narcotics violations constitute victimless crimes, the term is not without its ambiguities. Laws regulating such behavior undoubtedly view society or the "common good" as the victims of such offenses. So the term "victimless crimes" as typically used is value-laden.

Alcoholism and other forms of drug abuse are serious and socially disruptive psychological and perhaps medical problems; the law compounds this by making them legal problems first and foremost. While some have argued that individuals have a right to do with their bodies as they desire, our concern here is not so much with what ultimate treatment, if any, alcoholics, narcotic addicts, and prostitutes should receive, but with the fact that prosecution of such persons has important implications for other forms of criminality. The prosecution of crimes of morality impedes the police and other law-enforcement agencies from pursuing more serious kinds of crime, such as violent, business, and political crime which have widespread effects on vast numbers of people, and is seen as arbitrary and capricious by the groups most often prosecuted—women, the young, and the poor. This leads to unfavorable attitudes toward the police, resentment and distrust of them, and failure to cooperate with them, all of which reduce the overall effectiveness of the law as an instrument of social control and of law-enforcement agents as deterrents to crime.

In recent years there has been increasing pressure to legalize a variety of victimless crimes. The repeal of laws making offenses of gambling, marijuana and narcotics use, pornography, and prostitution and other sexual acts between consenting adults, has been called for, usually on the grounds that since so many people violate the existing laws, fair and impartial law enforcement is impossible. Morris and Hawkins (1970) argue that the "overreach" of the law may *contribute* to crime by creating inflated prices for illicit items, such as narcotics, which fosters organized crime and exposes the police to bribes. Problems associated with victimless crimes may be seen most dramatically in the case of narcotics, such as heroin.

Heroin and Crime

It is impossible to determine precisely the number of heroin addicts in the United States, but estimates of their number range from about 100,000 to several hundred thousand. In order to maintain their narcotics usage, they must each spend well over $100 a day for heroin. The means by which these vast sums of money are obtained are largely through selling drugs to others, stealing, prostitution, forgery, and occasionally, mugging (Markham, 1973). About 10 percent of all arrests for nondrug offenses involve drug addicts (Bureau of Justice Statistics, 1983).

Partly responsible for the criminal behavior of drug addicts— particularly robbery—has been our unwillingness as a nation to deal with drug dependency on any but a criminal level. Only when drug abuse became widespread in nonghetto areas of our cities was any concern shown for educative and rehabilitative programs, and even then there was great resistance to stripping away the criminal label and sanctions associated with drug dependency. The consequence of our failure to dissociate drugs from criminality has been to maintain and strengthen the link between the two. The undesirable effects of criminal penalties for drug use include undermining the stability of the user's family, reluctance of users to seek treatment, undermining respect for the law, maintaining an inflated price for heroin, exerting pressure on the user to enlist new users, maintaining organized crime, inhibiting research on drug effects and treatment of dependency, and causing death and disease through the sale of adulterated drugs and the use of unsterilized paraphernalia. "It is probably not an exaggeration to say that if one set out to design a system guaranteed to continually increase the rate of addiction, our present system would be somewhere near optimal" (Stachnik, 1972, p. 639).

To envision the consequences of our present means of dealing with drug dependency, an example taken from Lessard (1971) will be useful. Imagine that the 200,000 diabetics in the United States were suddenly told that insulin was illegal and that there were severe penalties for the possession, sale, or use of insulin. Would they become less dependent on the drug? Would they stop use of insulin because it was criminal? The probable effects of such a law would be to create an underground network of manufacture, distribution, and sale of insulin, not unlike the present heroin underworld. The price of insulin on the black market would rise dramatically, requiring the diabetic to obtain large sums of money, large enough to force him or her into further criminal activities in many cases. In time, the diabetic would be indistinguishable from our present-day heroin user.

Diabetics are currently indistinguishable from the rest of the population; they have no difficulty in supporting their families, holding jobs, and avoiding the stigma of being labeled dangerous criminals largely because insulin is freely available to them at reasonable cost.

While everything should be done to discourage a would-be user from dependency on narcotics, removal of penalties for drug use would go a long way in ameliorating the inevitable connection between drugs and other forms of crime. The adoption of a system not very different from the British system of heroin maintenance would (1) remove criminal penalties for the possession and use of all drugs, (2) provide methadone or heroin to any dependent user upon request, and (3) provide educational, psychological, and occupational therapy upon request. Far from costing more money than our present system, the proposed maintenance and therapeutic program would be far less costly in terms of personnel needs. It would save lives by eliminating accidental overdoses, check the spread of drug-related diseases, such as hepatitis and septicemia, and enable the user to dissociate him or herself from a criminal underworld. This in turn would reduce urban crime by anywhere from 15 to 50 percent (Stachnik, 1972).

Victimless crimes do not have much to do with public safety or well-being, but instead reflect middle-class morality. Because public sentiment toward moral issues changes more rapidly than legislation, laws about drinking, sex, gambling, and drug abuse inevitably reflect an earlier and generally more conservative view of public morality and order. Enforcement of these laws is a drain of increasingly scarce resources. Furthermore, the police should be freed from such duties as directing traffic, writing parking tickets, registering bicycles and taxis, running ambulance services, and rescuing stranded cats from trees so that their training and expertise are used to enforce laws with broader social consequences.

Additional Short-Term Remedies

The criminal justice system consists of three sometimes interrelated subsystems: police, courts, and corrections. Suggestions for changes in the functioning of these systems are based on the belief that a generally positive attitude toward the law and law enforcement is more likely to deter crime than the particular threats and penalties used as sanctions.

The Police. The President's Commission on Law Enforcement and Administration of Justice (1968) offered suggestions for improving police effectiveness and impartiality, some of which are consistent with the psychological research presented in earlier chapters of this book. Included among their 35 recommendations are the following:

Establish community relations units in departments serving substantial minority populations.

Establish citizen advisory committees in minority-group neighborhoods.

Recruit more minority-group officers.

Emphasize community relations in training and operations.

Provide adequate procedures for processing citizen grievances against all public officials.

Recruit more actively, especially on college campuses and in inner cities.

Increase police salaries, especially maximums, to competitive levels.

Set as goal, requirement of baccalaureate degree for general enforcement officers.

Stress ability in promotion.

Develop and enunciate policy guidelines for exercise of law enforcement discretion.

Establish strong internal investigation units in all departments to maintain police integrity.

Experiment with team policing combining patrol and investigative duties.

Adopt policy limiting use of firearms by officers. (pp. 653–655)

Others have called for similar measures (e.g., National Advisory Commission on Civil Disorders, 1968). The psychological consequences of such measures would be to reduce the social distance between the police and the community at large by removing some of the discretionary powers which the police now have. This may be accomplished by setting official limits on acceptable police conduct and by providing citizens with a nonpolice grievance board. Additional measures which would reduce the intrusiveness of the police would be to reinstate foot patrols and simultaneously reduce the number of patrol cars in any given neighborhood and to require police officers to live in the neighborhoods to which they are assigned.

The Courts.   Nearly 40 specific recommendations for changes in the operations of the court system were made by the President's Commission on Law Enforcement and Administration of Justice (1968), and a number of others have called for a variety of changes in the structure and operation of the courts:

Increase judicial manpower.

Enact comprehensive state bail reform legislation.

Establish station house release and summons procedure.

Revise sentencing provisions of penal codes.

Establish probation services in all courts for presentence investigation of every offender.

Institute procedures for promoting just and uniform sentencing.
Institute timetable for completion of criminal cases. (pp. 655–657)

Two additional changes can be recommended: elimination of the indeterminate sentence and elimination of secretive plea-bargaining.

These suggestions for uniform sentencing procedures are designed to ensure speedy trials and to eliminate the biases now built into the present court system against the indigent. For example, wealthy defendants are easily able to arrange bail while awaiting trial, while the poor must await trial in jail (Pines, 1973). Mitford (1973) summarizes the statistics from the Federal Bureau of Prisons records which "show that in 1970 the average sentence for whites was 42.9 months, compared to 57.5 months for nonwhites. Whites convicted of income tax evasion were committed for an average of 12.8 months and nonwhites for 28.6 months. In drug cases, the average for whites was 61.1 months and for nonwhites, 81.1." The need to revise sentencing provisions for criminal violations can also be seen in the wide variety of special-interest laws enacted in local and state legislatures and in the vast discrepancies in sentences from one locality to another for the same offense. In Colorado, for example, a person convicted of first-degree murder must serve at least 10 years before becoming eligible for parole, while a person convicted of second-degree murder must serve at least 15 years before becoming eligible for parole. In the same state, stealing a dog is punishable by up to 10 years' imprisonment, while killing a dog is punishable by no more than 6 months' imprisonment (President's Commission, 1968). Courts and laws which deal unevenly and prejudicially toward large segments of the population diminish respect for law in general and thereby foster crime.

Starr (1985) has offered suggestions for coping with urban crime. He notes that each city must determine for itself what its prime target will be in an effort to reduce crime. In New

York City the transportation system might be the first subject of attention. In Miami it might be drug-related crime, and San Antonio might choose to focus on border violations and ensuing violence. He calls for alternative punishment for first offenses and prison sentences for subsequent offenses. "There must be enough parts in a criminal court to hear a case expeditiously, to give the defendant a chance to speak on his own behalf, to listen to his counsel, and to make him see by their actions that the courts know who he is and what he did, and will be prepared for him even better when and if he does it again."

Corrections. Perhaps no area of the criminal justice system is in as much need of revision as correctional facilities. As discussed earlier, prison sentences are not necessarily rehabilitative, and in the long run they may even fail to protect society from crime.

Mitford has suggested that the very nature of prison may be such as to preclude long-term rehabilitation. The role of prisoner may be dehumanizing to the extent that true efforts at rehabilitation are unlikely or unable to succeed. Indeed, Haney, Banks, and Zimbardo (1973) have shown in their study of a simulated prison that both guards and prisoners are influenced more by the total context of prison, that is, by their expectations of what prisons are and what happens in them, than by the specific attitudes and personalities of either guards or inmates. In their study, men were randomly assigned to be either prisoners or prison guards. Within only a few days the experiment had to be terminated because of the excessive abuse to which "prisoners" were exposed at the hands of the "guards."

There are several remedial steps that could be taken to ensure that, at the very least, correctional institutions do not serve to teach and reinforce antisocial behavior.

In G. K. Chesterton's *The Club of Queer Trades,* a judge must pass sentence on a prisoner at the bar: "I sentence you to three years' penal servitude, in the firm and God-given convic-

tion that what you really require is three weeks at the seaside."
While prison reform has repeatedly been called for over the
past hundred years, no successful efforts to deal humanely with
convicts have ever been instituted on a wide scale. As a necessary beginning, the adversary nature of the institution must be
weakened. Prisoners working in conjunction with administrators and other prison and community personnel must be made
to feel a part of the society at large rather than apart from it.
By assigning at least some of the responsibility for rehabilitation to the prisoners themselves, commitment to acceptable
social behavior can be increased. Prison administrators need to
have available a variety of positive incentives for prisoners to
encourage acceptable forms of social behavior, rather than the
presently existing punishments consisting primarily of isolation
and parole denials for antisocial conduct. A variety of supportive facilities is required for prisoners, such as job training,
education, and psychological counseling. Prison facilities should
be small, community-based operations and should use the support facilities available in the surrounding community whenever
possible. Rather than isolating the prisoner from his or her
family, efforts should be taken to strengthen the family structure in the form of graduated release programs and expanded
furlough programs. At present, only 5 percent of the total
prison budget is for rehabilitative services.

These reforms are hardly original, since they—or reforms like
them—have been called for almost since prisons began. As Mitford has shown, however, they have never been instituted. One
reason for resistance may be that prisons are so crowded with
such a great variety of offenders that reform efforts seem sec-
ondary to the more mundane requirements of housing, feeding,
and controlling the large number of people. The Board of Di-
rectors of the National Council on Crime and Delinquency
(1973) has suggested that this problem be alleviated by providing "nondangerous offenders" with sentences not involving
prison. They have urged the courts to use treatment by appropriate social agencies, probation, suspended sentences, "de-

ferred conviction," fines, restitution, boarding homes, and half-way houses as alternative to prison sentences for all those convicted of crimes other than serious personal and organized crimes. That such programs are feasible can be seen from the fact that even prison administrators agree that between 75 and 90 percent of all prisoners would, if freed immediately, present no danger or threat to the community (Milford, 1973). This is consistent with the literature (discussed in Chapter 3) showing that so many crimes, including personal crimes, are committed by relatively average people in rather atypical situations, rather than by atypical people in normal situations.

Behavioral Intervention

While situational factors are seen largely as the determinants of aggression and crime, certain psychological traits of some individuals make them more likely to aggress in what I have called aggressible environments. Among the psychological characteristics are impulsivity, loss of cognitive control over behavior, deindividuation, inability to delay gratification, an extensive aggressive repertoire, and a restricted range of alternative (non-aggressive) behaviors.

One way to curtail aggressive behavior is to structure the environment in such a way as to minimize the opportunity for aggression. However, since most violence is committed against persons familiar or friendly to the aggressor, no matter how the environment it altered, it would neither be possible nor desirable to minimize contact with familiar people or places, to instate cognitive control over certain behavior, or to maximize surveillance of some areas. Since cognitive controls are relaxed in a familiar environment and in the presence of familiar others, some probability of engaging in aggression is always present in these situations. In order to reduce this probability, individuals can and should learn to maintain control over their behavior and have a wide range of behavioral alternatives other than aggression in which to engage.

Particularly important for a reduction in criminal aggression is the provision of alternative behaviors for juveniles who have already shown signs of criminality or excessive violence. The types of training that may be expected to reduce antisocial behavior include increasing the individual's ability to foresee the consequences of his or her actions and increasing the ability to verbalize, rather than act out (Goldstein & Rosenbaum, 1982). There is quite a large number of intervention studies with juvenile delinquents, and a sampling of such studies is presented in order to indicate the variety of approaches which have met with success in reducing antisocial acts.

In one study (Chandler, 1973), chronically delinquent boys were taught to place themselves in the positions of other people by making a film in which they had to enact a variety of different roles. This role-taking procedure was designed to reduce the egocentrism of the boys. A placebo group made an animated film but did not engage in role-taking, and a control group made no film at all. The results of the study indicate that enacting the roles of a variety of others did reduce egocentrism. The experimental group showed a significant reduction in delinquent offenses in the 18 months following the film-making exercise, while no such reduction in delinquency was observed for the placebo or the control group.

A study by Alexander and Parsons (1973) involved the fostering of communication and negotiation skills among members of delinquents' families. Recidivism rates for delinquents in these experimental families were compared with those delinquents receiving client-centered family therapy, church-sponsored family counseling, or no treatment. The results of the study showed that the lowest recidivism rate (26 percent) was for those delinquents who, along with their families, received instruction in communicating and negotiating, while the highest recidivism rate (73 percent) was for those receiving the family counseling. The recidivism rates for the client-centered groups

(47 percent) and the no-treatment groups (50 percent) were about the same as the recidivism rate for the county as a whole (51 percent). Hence, as the authors conclude, "it appears that family intervention programs may profitably be focused on changing family interaction patterns in the direction of increased clarity and precision of communication, increased reciprocity of communication and social reinforcement, and contingency contracting emphasizing equivalence of rights and responsibilities for all family members" (p. 224). One effect of the family intervention technique employed by Alexander and Parsons may have been, as in the Chandler study on role-taking, to increase the delinquents' ability to view things from the perspective of others. This would in turn decrease impulsivity and the tendency to engage in self-centered behavior.

The importance of communication in reducing antisocial behavior is further highlighted by Ostrom, Steele, Rosenblood, and Mirels (1971):

> By the time a youth is labeled a "juvenile delinquent" by society, he is likely to have developed a resistance to the conventional means society uses to transmit values and encourage law-abiding behavior. The school teacher punishes him for misbehavior in the hallways and classrooms, the judge instructs him to "mend his ways," a probation officer counsels him to keep off the streets and avoid "bad" company, parents scold, and ministers preach. He has become an inert and unreceptive agent in this communication process. Treatment programs for the abatement of delinquent behavior which do not alter this communication pattern have little chance of being effective. (p. 119)

Ostrom and his colleagues conducted an intervention study with delinquents who had been placed on probation by the juvenile court. A variety of social psychological principles were applied. Leaders of the intervention groups were selected and trained so that they would be familiar with the delinquents' problems and life styles and could be easily identified with by the delinquents. The subjects were recruited through the courts in such a way as to maximize each person's feeling of choice: the subjects were told that they would be released from mandatory visits with parole officers if they agreed to serve as "consultants in a project designed to understand 'why kids get into trouble.'" Attendance at the experimental sessions was purely voluntary since "making participation a compulsory requirement can destroy the effectiveness of influence attempts." The 2-hour sessions were held weekly for 2 months. During the sessions, the subjects discussed delinquency, the consequences of delinquent acts, and alternative means of achieving the participants' personal goals. A variety of role-playing procedures was used in which participants took the role of parents, arresting officers, victims, law breakers, judges, jailers, school teachers, gang leaders, and innocent bystanders. In order to increase the boys' commitment during these role-playing sessions, videotape recordings were made which were viewed and discussed. The boys were rewarded with a letter of praise for behavior which was self-initiated and internally motivated. A control group of delinquents received no such treatment.

School and court records were examined during the 10 months immediately following the experimental sessions, and at the end of this 10 month follow-up subjects were given a variety of paper and pencil measures to determine whether the treatment sessions had any lasting influence on values or attitudes. Nearly twice as many members of the control group (48 percent) as the experimental group (26 percent) committed at least one delinquent act during the 10 months following the sessions. During the first 4 months after the sessions, 50 percent of the control group, as compared to 8 percent of the experimental group, had at least one arrest. The difference between the experimental and control groups diminished with the passage of time, indicating the need for longer-term intervention sessions or the occasional reinstatement of the treatment. Subjects in the experimental group, however, did show a lasting increase in self-supportive attitudes.

A number of intervention studies have altered the consequence of aggressive behavior by withholding rewards for aggression and by providing rewards for alternative, nonaggressive behavior (Hawkins, Peterson, Schweid, & Bijou, 1966; Patterson, Cobb, & Ray, 1973). Such studies have been fairly successful in diminishing antisocial behavior among delinquents. One of the bases for the Big Brother and Big Sister programs, in which a delinquent youth is paired with an older nondelinquent, usually a student, is that the Big Brother or Sister will serve as a model to the delinquent and will reward prosocial behavior while ignoring or disapproving of antisocial behavior.

While the various programs outlined above might reduce street crime, auto theft, or recidivism among criminals and deliquents, they leave untouched the basic core of aggression—the acquisition of aggressive and antisocial values, attitudes, and behaviors. The remedial programs suggested so far are capable of reducing antisocial behavior among people who have already acquired a basic aggressive repertoire. However, without fundamental changes in what we learn and the ways in which we learn them, it is only a matter of time before the effectiveness of such remedial measures diminishes.

6
Toward
Elimination of
Violence

Crime moves downward in the social structure. Through their deeds, individuals who control resources and who are widely admired have a disproportionate influence on others. When crimes occur in upper levels of society, in government, business, and entertainment, observers learn and may be instigated to imitate criminal behavior. Since so many crimes are crimes of opportunity, individuals will commit, not necessarily the same crimes as those they observe, but those that are most readily available to them in their day-to-day lives. Often these are crimes of violence.

> Crime is a social problem that is interwoven with almost every aspect of American life; controlling it involves changing the way schools are run and classes are taught, the way cities are planned and built, the way businesses are managed and workers are hired. Crime is a kind of human behavior; controlling it means changing the minds and hearts of men. Controlling crime is the business of every American institution. Controlling crime is the business of every American. (President's Commission, 1968, p. 642)

One method of curtailing violence, and particularly violent crime, is to reduce the degree of pro-violence attitudes and actions in social institutions. The extent to which the family, schools, government, and the entertainment industry rely upon and exploit real or threatened violence is astounding. It is unlikely that the problem of violence in American society can be redressed until nonviolent, alternative means of rearing children, conducting foreign policy, and spending leisure time are found.

Removing Rewards For Violence

Three essential forms of learning aggression were discussed in Chapter 2: classical conditioning, operant conditioning, and social learning or imitation. If these learning approaches are applied to the elimination of violence then the juxtaposition of violence with ethnic, national, religious, or racial groups needs to be avoided (classical conditioning), rewards for violence should be removed (operant conditioning), and the modeling of aggression in the social environment needs to be minimized (social learning).

The reward structure in relation to violence can be altered in several ways. One is to increase the personal costs of violence, primarily through public and judicial condemnation (Brier & Piliavin, 1965; Piliavin, Hardyck, & Vadum, 1968), another is to decrease the positive reinforcements for engaging in violence, and a third is to provide alternative ways of arriving at desirable goals without resorting to violence.

Parent-Rearing

It is during childhood that the underlying core of aggressive behavior and related attitudes, values, and norms are acquired. Parental behavior is the greatest influence on this learning. Parents who praise aggression at least in some forms, those who directly or indirectly reward aggressive behavior, and parents who themselves are aggressive teach aggression to their children. When parents also show a lack of affection, concern, and understanding toward their children, such learning is even more pronounced.

Several of the studies of behavioral intervention mentioned in the previous chapter show that when parents of deliquent youths are provided with such skills as how to reward and punish behavior correctly and how to exchange ideas and feelings with their children, improvements in the children's behavior soon follow. Of course, it is not only the parents of deliquent youths who might profit from improved child-rearing skills; nearly all parents, often inadvertently, teach their children some antisocial behaviors and values.

Many of the major elements of successful child-rearing historically have been present in most families: tenderness, affection, concern, understanding. But also present were inconsistencies in behavior, the modeling of aggression and praise for particular instances of violence, which provided children, if not with propensities to engage in violence, at least with pro-aggression values and behaviors that would find expression under appropriate circumstances.

While high school and college courses are offered in the films of Woody Allen, volleyball, advertising, and cooking, none is offered in how to raise a child. This is not true of some countries, such as China and the Soviet Union, in which training in moral behavior, concern for family, and social skills are taught throughout the school system (Bronfenbrenner, 1970). Students need instruction throughout their education in the philosophy and psychology of parenthood. Such instruction need not be ideological, as is the Soviet teaching of social and moral skills, but can provide students with an understanding of the functions of parenthood and with a variety of social and psychological skills that will enable them to raise their children in an intelligent, purposive, and effective manner.

There are already some programs of "parenting skills" for parents and would-be parents offered by pediatric hospitals and behavior therapy clinics throughout the United States. These offer the student lessons in the psychology of child development, the effective uses of reward and punishment, and the development of social skills, such as the communication of attitudes and feelings.

Child abuse would be sharply reduced if parents had available a variety of nonaggressive strategies from which they could choose when dealing with their children. In many American cities, crisis centers have established 24-hour telephone "hot lines" to provide counseling and expert advice to parents. Even the awareness of such a resource may be sufficient to reduce child abuse. In one laboratory study (Goldstein, Davis, Kernis, & Cohn, 1981), the mere presence of a telephone hotline reduced the amount of punishment administered by college men in a learning setting.

There is a growing awareness among teachers and parents that it is detrimental to children to teach them stereotypic sex-role behavior. For example, it will not be to a girl's benefit to learn submission and passivity since this may undermine her initiative in pursuing an education, a career, or other personal goals. The compensating tendency may be to raise girls in the same way that boys have been reared previously. This would have the long-term effect of increasing overt aggressiveness among females. Of course it is possible to minimize sexism in child-rearing without at the same time encouraging aggression or pro-aggression attitudes and values.

The psychologist Nevitt Sanford (1971), one of the authors of the classic *Authoritarian Personality,* noted that "For turning our culture in the direction of humane and democratic values nothing is more important than reform of our schools. Nobody knows how this reform is to be accomplished, but we can offer some suggestions. Although schools probably need some structure, they certainly do not have to be authoritarian. The authoritarian style . . . is not inherent in human nature but is a patterned reaction to circumstances" (pp. 316–317). Therefore, not only can schools encourage the development of positive parental and social skills, but by becoming less structured they provide the students with a more active and responsible role to play, the effects of which would be to enhance

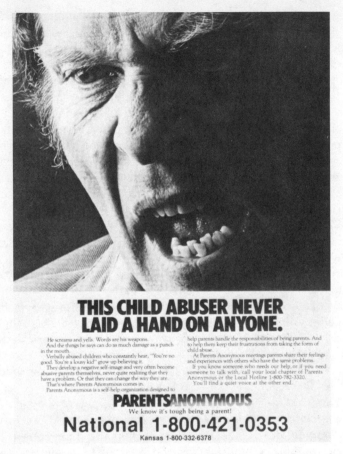

Figure 6.1 Child abuse may be verbal as well as physical. Reprinted by permission.

their sense of autonomy and acceptance of responsibility for their decisions.

The Mass Media

An American child typically watches television for more than 27 hours per week. By age 16 the average child will have seen

200,000 acts of violence and 50,000 attempted murders (*NCTV News,* 1985). Violence in mass media teaches pro-aggression values and behaviors and in specific instances may instigate individual acts of violence. It provides heavy viewers with a distorted picture of the real world and makes them inured to violence and crime (Cline, Croft, & Courrier, 1973). Perhaps the most pernicious effect of media violence is the implicit support it lends to aggression by portraying fictional heroes as relying on violence for the resolution of conflict.

Televised sports also emphasize and reward violence (Bryant & Zillmann, 1983) and portray an exaggerated set of stereotypically masculine values (Goldstein & Bredemeier, 1977; Prisuta, 1979). The reduction of sports violence is used as an example of the strategies for reducing violence that have been proposed by social scientists. Similar sorts of proposals have been made with regard to other forms of media violence.

Reducing Sports Violence

As with love, the expression of aggression does not diminish the capacity for subsequent expression but instead enhances it. Violence in sports, whether among athletes or fans, is hardly a harmless outlet for pent-up frustration. In Chapter 2 we reviewed research on the extent and effects of sports-related violence. Methods for its reduction are reviewed here.

In general, suggestions for reducing sports violence fall into two categories: external constraints and internal restraints. External constraints involve situational changes that would make violence less appealing and more difficult for would-be aggressors. Among the constraints proposed (by Williams, Dunning, & Murphy, 1984; Yaeger, 1979, among others) are the following:

- Changes in the rules and stricter enforcement of the rules concerning violence among athletes and fans.
- Changing the temporal aspects of sporting events, such as instituting postgame concerts or the playing of several games

in succession, so that the spectators do not all leave at once.
• Restricting the sale or availability of alcoholic beverages.
• Changes in equipment to protect athletes better.
• Redesign of playing fields, such as the pitch at European soccer fields, to minimize fan-player contact and to minimize riots among spectators.
• Increase show of force by police.
• Reduce focus on violence by sports journalists and broadcasters.

These short-term remedies do not alter the motivation of an individual to engage in violence, but instead simply make it more difficult and less inviting to do so. Nevertheless, external constraints are quick and workable solutions to a social problem of some magnitude. To reduce aggressive motivation, however, requires long-term strategies.

Internal restraints consist of fundamental changes in the attitudes, values, and perceptions of athletes, broadcasters, sports management, and fans. Internal restraints are self-imposed inhibitions on aggression and a lowered tolerance for the aggressive behavior of others. Such long-term changes can come about only by emphasizing the nonviolent aspects of body-contact sports, the role of cooperation, aesthetics, and the prosocial aspects of competitive athletics (see Goldstein, 1983; 1985b).

News coverage of violence and terrorism may also teach and instigate acts of violence (Phillips & Hensley, 1984; Schmid & de Graaf, 1982). Berkowitz and Macaulay (1971) found that following both the assassination of President John F. Kennedy in November 1963 and the multiple murders by Richard Speck and Charles Whitman in 1966 there were unusually sharp increases in the number of violent crimes committed. Further, Payne and Payne (1970) reported a decrease in crime during a newspaper strike in Detroit, suggesting that the reporting of crime stimulates further crime.

There are sensitive issues raised by these findings and by those reported in Chapter 2. On the one hand, since evidence indicates that violence in the mass media serves in several ways to increase aggression, crime, and terrorism, the elimination of violence in the media may reduce criminal violence. On the other hand, if certain media content are censored they are apt to become more attractive and more valued by people (Brock, 1968; Fromkin & Brock, 1973), and in any event, censorship is hardly an acceptable means of controlling media content in a democratic society. What may be effective in minimizing media portrayal of violence and curtailing its impact on the aggressive behavior of viewers is to inform people of the effects of such portrayals and to apply economic pressure to sponsors of violent media programming. Organizations such as the National Coalition on Television Violence monitor and attempt to influence the level of violence in mass media.

The National Commission on the Causes and Prevention of Violence (1968) recommended several years ago that "the broadcasting of children's cartoons containing serious non-comic violence should be abandoned. . . . The amount of time devoted to the broadcast of crime, western, and action-adventure programs containing violent episodes should be reduced" (pp. 172–173). Such voluntary regulation has not been forthcoming from the broadcast industry. The major television networks claim that they would not present violent programming so often if they did not receive such high Nielsen ratings. *TV Guide* reported (5–11 January 1974) the following:

> It was the old, old rating story again: on the night of December 16, while more than two out of three TV homes across the country watched one of two regular crime-chasing dramas (39 percent of the audience tuned in *Columbo,* another 29 percent *Mannix*) a mere 25 percent of the viewers chose to catch the rare TV appearance of Katherine Hepburn in ABC's critically applauded *The Glass Menagerie.*

What the networks and the above fail to take into account are two factors. First, if people are accustomed to watching enormous quantities of violence on television, they will come to prefer violent programs. Second, if people are apathetic about what they view on TV, they might simply choose at random which programs to watch. The ratings referred to in the *TV Guide* report reflect a random distribution which indicates no particular preference among viewers at all (we would expect about one-third of the viewers to tune in each network).

Not only do people learn and imitate the antisocial behavior they see on television and in films, they also learn and imitate the prosocial behavior they see. An increase in the portrayal of positive social behaviors would both teach and encourage similar behaviors among viewers (Baron, 1971; Bryan & Test, 1967) and might also reduce the negative impact of aggressive programming (Holper, Goldstein, & Snyderman, 1974; Huesmann, Eron, Klein, Brice, & Fischer, 1983). This viewpoint underlies some of the children's programming on public television.

The reporting of factual events, such as airplane hijackings and interpersonal violence, may also contribute to the learning and performance of aggression and crime. Censorship of news media is hardly necessary to curb the social-learning effects of media violence, however. Crime and violence can be presented in such a way that they do not appear to be desirable, justified, or without serious consequences. This statement rests on the belief that any event can be described in many ways, that there is no single "objective" method of reporting. Descriptions can be chosen to present events in a manner consistent with the public interest. (See also suggestions concerning media violence in Johnson, 1967.)

The way we speak of events influences what we do about them. Irving Janis (1971) describes decision-making during the Lyndon Johnson administration:

> When the in-group of key advisers met with Johnson every Tuesday, their meetings were characterized by a games theory detachment concerning the consequences of the war policies they were discussing. The members of this group adopted a special vocabulary for describing the Vietnam war, using

terms such as body counts, armed reconnaissance, and surgical strikes, which they picked up from their military colleagues. The Vietnam policy makers, by using this professional military vocabulary, were able to avoid in their discussions with each other all direct references to human suffering and thus to form an attitude of detachment similar to that of surgeons. But although an attitude of detachment may have functional value for those who must execute distressing operations, it makes it all too easy for policy makers to dehumanize the victims of war and to resort to destructive military solutions without considering their human consequences. (pp. 73–74)

The labels with which one thinks about events come to have a strong influence on *what* one thinks about them.

Reducing Institutionalized Modeling of Aggression

In the same way that rewards for aggression portrayed in the mass media foster aggression and related values, so too does antisocial behavior committed by those prominent in public affairs. Aggression and criminal behavior by those in the upper social strata strengthen and instigate similar acts by others in the society. For example, the mayor of a large American city admitted at a press conference that he had members of the local police department assemble dossiers on local judges. When asked whether that wasn't a violation of the Constitution, he answered that, even if it was, he would continue to have the police maintain the dossiers (*New York Times,* 5 August 1973). Such blatant disregard for the law can only reduce respect for the law among observers. Likewise, political scandals involving officials in the highest levels of government undermine respect for the law and thereby increase the likelihood that other citizens will engage in criminal activities.

It is not only government officials involved in criminal activities who lend support to criminality; what has generally been referred to as business- or white-collar-crime also reinforces and sets examples for other types of illegal conduct. The extent of such crime, while it is difficult to determine precisely, far exceeds in economic and social impact the more readily detectable forms of street crime reported by the FBI in its annual Uniform Crime Reports. In their criminology text, Bloch and Geis (1962) discuss the varieties of white-collar crime, ranging from advertising fraud, violations of anti-trust legislation, and income-tax evasion, to overcharges on automobile, electrical appliances, and watch repairs. In a classic study of business crime, E. H. Sutherland (1949) examined the top 70 corporations in the United States and found that nearly 1,000 adverse decisions had been rendered against them by courts or administrative bodies, with at least one decision against each of the 70 corporations.

> Financial losses due to white-collar crime . . . are probably many times as great as the financial cost of all acts customarily included in the so-called "crime problem." An officer of a chain grocery store, for instance, embezzled $600,000 in one year, a figure six times higher than the annual losses from five hundred robberies and burglaries in the stores in that chain. Million-dollar burglaries or robberies are virtually unknown, and constitute national sensations, where a million-dollar embezzlement is a rather routine event. (p. 383)

The question has been raised by some legal scholars and criminologists as to whether white-collar crimes should be considered crimes at all. They hold that many white-collar crimes involve torts, or infractions of the civil law, rather than violations of the criminal law. While there may be legal and historical reasons to distinguish between white-collar and personal crimes, there is less psychological justification to do so. Any action which an individual chooses to perform that is designed to injure, physically or psychologically, another person is an aggressive act. We have not previously distinguished between aggressive acts which are legal and those which are illegal, nor between those which are direct (physical) and those which are indirect (psychological); they differ largely in degree and are essentially similar in other respects. The fact that one man accosts another on the street in order to obtain his money, while a second sells Florida swampland as an "ideal spot for a vacation home" in order to obtain the buyer's money does not make one actor significantly less aggressive than the other. Some acts of aggression are legal and others illegal, but I have chosen to treat them in a similar fashion. One further reason for treating them together is because it can be argued that the amount of legal aggression which exists in a society is highly related to the amount of illegal violence which exists. The more tolerant a society is of various kinds of acceptable (legal) violence, as in child-rearing, play, humor, sports, politics, entertainment, and daily social intercourse, the more likely it will be to have high rates of criminal violence since the former serve largely as training grounds for the latter. If a society is saturated with petty violence, it is sure to have a high degree of criminal violence as well; and if a society is saturated with criminal behavior among its ruling elite, it will be flooded with crime among its masses (cf. Nader, 1985).

Public concern over crime is generally restricted to those crimes which are reflected in the Uniform Crime Reports of the FBI. Listed as "serious crimes" in the reports are murder, rape, robbery, aggravated assault, burglary, larceny ($50 and over), and auto theft. These are, of course, matters that concern the public and the police; but many crimes committed on less personal bases, such as white-collar crimes, are no less (perhaps even more) serious in their consequences. If the Uniform Crime Reports are maintained in the future, and if they are to be used as an index of crime in the United States, then they should accurately reflect the spectrum of crime, including those committed by middle- and upper-class citizens in addition to those committed by the poor, young, and nonwhite.

The Uniform Crime Reports rely on those crimes that are reported to the police, and therefore, they are highly dependent upon the willingness of citizens to report crime and on the accounting methods used by the various police departments across the nation. A more accurate index of the extent of crime is obtained from interviews conducted with nationwide random samples of citizens. Of primary importance is that the public and law-enforcement agencies expand their conception of and concern about crime to encompass the whole range of serious infringements on individual and social liberties.

War and Psychology

A theory of aggression, if it is sound enough, ought to be capable of explaining, and perhaps predicting, wars between nations. In addition, a good theory should carry implications for the reduction of violence. The theories and research reviewed to this point have generally been limited to aggression between two people. We may ask whether frustration-aggression theory, psychoanalytic theory, or social-learning theory have anything to tell us about international aggression.

Before we begin a brief review of these theories with reference to war and peace, something should be said about this approach to the topic. I do not believe that a complete and ultimate understanding of war is to be found in psychology, but war requires a psychological explanation to some extent, since it is the result of human judgment, values, and decisions. Several years ago a large university hosted an interdisciplinary symposium on war. The panel consisted of a distinguished economist, a political scientist, a psychologist, and a sociologist, each of whom gave a brief talk on the causes of war. The economist saw war as largely caused by social factors such as poverty and alienation. The psychologist thought that wars were fought primarily over economic issues. The political scientist believed that the personalities of national leaders led to war, that they were psychologically caused. And the sociologist thought wars were caused by conflicting political ideologies. Each expert believed that the best explanation of war was to be found in someone else's bailiwick, perhaps because none of them was very confident that his own discipline presented a satisfactory explanation. War is little studied in psychology, but that does not obviate the role that psychology plays in its occurrence (see Allen, 1985; Morawski & Goldstein, 1985).

Frustration as a Cause of War

In examining the frustration-aggression theory within the context of nations rather than individuals, it is necessary to distinguish between two types of political violence: revolutionary violence within a country and international warfare between two or more countries. Frustration-aggression theory has more often been applied to the former than the latter.

In perhaps the best studies of frustration and revolutionary violence, Ivo Feierabend, a political scientist, and Rosalind Feierabend, a social psychologist, examined various sources of frustration and their effects on violence within political entities (1966, 1972). For 84 nations they obtained information on such variables as the percentage of the population that was literate, the number of radios, newspapers, and telephones per 1,000 people, the number of physicians in the nation, per capita income and GNP, and the percentage of the population living in rural and urban areas. They also obtained information on the degree of aggression within the country. They determined both the amount of aggression directed by individuals and groups within the political system against other groups or officeholders, and the amount of aggression directed by officeholders against others. Political violence includes strikes, riots, terrorist acts, mass political arrests, coups d'état, and political executions.

Frustration in this research was defined as unsatisfied needs, expectations, or aspirations of many people. This is, in fact, a definition of "relative deprivation" or "relative frustration" (Merton & Kitt, 1952); it considers a situation as frustrating when individuals are deprived of something they want or expect. Thus, of two nations with the same number of telephones per 1,000 population, only one of them may have high frustration because its people expect or want telephones, while the other may be low in frustration because people neither want nor expect phones. Feierabend and Feierabend reasoned that in countries with a largely urban population and a high degree of literacy, people would be aware of and consequently would expect, more phones, newspapers, medical attention, money, and food. In one study, Feierabend and Feierabend (1972) found that those countries with the greatest frustration levels also had the highest rate of political violence. (See Table 6.1.)

Does this way of conceptualizing frustration also account for international aggression? The Feierabends and Frank Scanland (1972) examined international hostility, including formal protests, accusations, expulsion of diplomats, troop movements, the severing of diplomatic relations, military actions, and declarations of war. For 53 nations in the period 1955–1960, the relative amount of internal frustration is positively correlated with international aggression ($r = +.33$). Not surprisingly, those countries exhibiting greatest internal violence also were the most externally aggressive ($r = +.52$).

To the extent that the Feierabends' conception of frustration is similar to that of Dollard and his colleagues (1939) in their initial version of frustration-aggression theory, we can conclude that both revolutionary violence within a country and warfare between countries are positively related to frustration. Unfortunately, this analysis of war does not provide a detailed description of the particular mechanisms that operate to determine revolutions or wars. For example, it does not tell us whether a high degree of internal violence follows or precedes international violence. It is conceivable that international acts of aggression are instrumentally employed to undermine internal revolutions by providing the population with a common focus in the form of a foreign enemy. Nor does the theory tell us which countries will be aggressed against. On the whole, however, the evidence indicates that the level of frustration of a

TABLE 6.1   Relationship Between Level of Frustration and Degree of Internal Violence

	High Frustration	Low Frustration
High internal violence	(34) Bolivia, Brazil, Bulgaria, Ceylon, Chile, Colombia, Cuba, Cyprus, Dom. Republic, Ecuador, Egypt, El Salvador, Greece, Guatemala, Haiti, India, Indonesia, Iran, Iraq, Italy, Japan, Korea, Mexico, Nicaragua, Pakistan, Panama, Paraguay, Peru, Spain, Syria, Thailand, Turkey, Venezuela, Yugoslavia	(6) Argentina, Belgium, France, Lebanon, Morocco, Union of South Africa
Low internal violence	(2) Philippines, Tunisia	(20) Australia, Austria, Canada, Costa Rica, Czechoslovakia, Denmark, Ireland, Israel, Netherlands, New Zealand, Norway, Portugal, Finland, West Germany, Great Britain, Iceland, Sweden, Switzerland, United States, Uruguay

Note: Data are for the period from 1948 to 1962.

Source: Adapted from "Systemic Conditions of Political Aggression: An Application of Frustration-aggression Theory" by I. K. Feierabend and R. L. Feierabend, 1972, in I. K. Feierabend, R. L. Feierabend, and T. R. Gurr (Eds.), *Anger, Violence, and Politics*, Englewood Cliffs, N.J.: Prentice-Hall. Used by permission.

nation's population is positively associated with both domestic and foreign aggression.

Psychoanalytic Theory

The psychoanalytic theory of war is loosely organized and largely untested. Freud discussed the causes of war briefly in several papers, most notably in *Civilization and Its Discontents* (1930) and in an exchange of views with Albert Einstein published as *Why War?* (1934). However, there are a number of Freudian-derived theories and analyses of war. Most psychoanalytic analyses of war involve three elements: unconscious motives, ego-defense mechanisms, and innate aggression.

Perhaps the major contribution of psychoanalytic theory to our understanding of human behavior is its emphasis on unconscious determinants of behavior. While there is much disagreement over how much behavior is unconsciously motivated, there is little doubt that some behaviors are caused by nonconscious motives. Ego-defense mechanisms function on an unconscious level. The familiar devices of rationalization, projection, displacement, denial, and identification act beneath the level of consciousness to protect the ego from threatening thoughts or feelings. Taking these two ideas together—unconscious motivation and ego-defense mechanisms—it is easy to understand how wars may be rationalized (Klineberg, 1964, 1984).

Nations do not perceive themselves as acting aggressively in war, but as acting defensively. People believe their nation is acting rationally and with good intentions when it engages in warfare. Each sees its opponents as acting irrationally and unjustly. It is never *we* who are aggressive and unreasonable, but because of *their* hostility we must act defensively. This state of affairs may be interpreted in terms of the ego-defense mechanisms of rationalization, projection, displacement, denial, and identification. Rationalization of aggression leads people to emphasize the evil qualities of the opponent (Hooton, 1937).

Farber (1955) has written of the role of displacement in war. An unconscious hatred of the father, the result of unresolved Oedipal conflict, "my be displaced onto strong authority figures and manifested specifically by a resentment against the United States on the part of a citizen of a weak country."

Denial may play an important role in international relations. Not only do citizens of a country deny their own nation's aggressiveness, but they deny the threat of warfare, particularly nuclear warfare, itself. What else enables us to look with fascination at films of mushroom clouds ascending over a nuclear test site? Or to view *The Day After* and do nothing the day after? The magnitude of a nuclear holocaust is unfathomable, an incomprehensibility that facilitates denial and inaction.

Anthony Brandt (1984) reports a conversation with a Jewish friend who said he could not feel anything for the 6 million Jews killed in the Holocaust. "They're just numbers," he explained. "I can't feel anything for numbers. If my father or mother had died, that's different. But six million? It doesn't register." Likewise, the projected consequences of a nuclear war are mere numbers. How does one imagine 120 million Americans, the likely death toll of a limited nuclear war? We need to do what we have never been able to do: imagine our own ends, and multiply that by the 4 or 5 billion people on earth, and all the other creatures besides.

Some psychoanalytic writers have suggested that international conflicts may reflect the need periodically to discharge a buildup of aggressive energy. But we have already seen (Chapter 1) that the notion of energy storage and discharge is misconceived.

It is difficult to test these ideas in a satisfactory way. It is clear that people tend to see their nation's behavior as justified in times of war, and that they see the enemy as aggressive and unjust. But this does not mean that these effects occur because of rationalization and projection. They may be explained by notions of cognitive consistency (Abelson et al., 1968). For example, it would be psychologically uncomfortable to live in a nation that had just sent troops to a foreign country for no apparent reason. Because private citizens cannot reduce this discomfort by recalling their nation's armies, they try to reduce it by providing some justification for the troops' deployment. Hence, the British support for the Falkland Islands war and American support for the invasion of Grenada. We do not need to invoke unconscious motives or processes to explain why people justify events that have already occurred and over which they have little control. Indeed, Festinger's (1957) cognitive dissonance theory is a simpler and more testable explanation.

War and Social-Learning Theory

Foreign policy is conducted as though nations, like individuals, have motives, desires, attitudes, and values. Even though this assumption is false it continues to guide the behavior of government leaders. Psychologically speaking, it doesn't matter whether the assumptions that guide behavior are valid: If they are true to the actor, they are real in their consequences.

If we adopt the assumption that nations possess the same basic characteristics as individuals, several ways of dealing with conflict suggest themselves. A nation, like an individual, serves as a model for other nations that observe its actions. One example of modeling by nations can be seen in the disproportionate influence that Scandinavian countries have on the domestic and foreign affairs of other nations, an influence that far exceeds their economic or military strength.

Like individuals, nations cannot hope to gain the support and trust of other nations through foreign aid or military power. Friendship is more apt to be earned than bought. Indeed, the research of Kenneth Gergen and his colleagues has shown that foreign aid may have undesirable consequences for international relations if it is not offered in a way that allows nations to save face and maintain a sense of autonomy. In their cross-cultural research, Gergen and his colleagues examined the recipients of aid (Gergen, Ellsworth, Maslach, & Seipel, 1975; Gergen, Morse, & Kristeller, 1973). In their studies, students in Japan, Korea, Scotland, South Africa, Sweden, Taiwan, and the United States were asked how they would feel about someone who offered to help them. Among the conditions varied were the amount of resources available to the donor, whether the donor required repayment of the aid, and whether there were restrictions on how the aid was to be used. They measured attraction to and liking for the donor and whether repayment would be made. There were no major differences between the students of different countries in evaluation of the donor or in the tendency to repay the donor. The donor was liked most when recipients were obliged to repay the aid. As the obligations attached to the aid increased, the recipients became more resistant to receiving it and more negative to their feelings toward the donor. Greater attraction was found for poor as opposed to wealthy donors. The desire to return money given in aid was greater for poor than for wealthy donors, regardless of whether repayment was originally demanded.

If, as social-learning theory suggests, a country serves as a social model, then it is obliged to act toward its own citizens as it would have other nations act. The way to propagate its own policies is to demonstrate in practice their utility and the extent to which those policies result in well-being. A nation whose leaders act with compassion is also attacking internal violence and crime in an effective fashion. Public officials, because their behavior is visible, serve as behavioral models for other citizens. If they model behaviors that we regard positively, others are apt to internalize these behaviors and follow suit.

Osgood's (1962) theory of international conflict-resolution, called Graduated and Reciprocated Initiatives in Tension-Reduction (or GRIT, for short), although it was not developed with social-learning theory in mind, is consistent with that more general approach. GRIT involves an "arms race in reverse." A nation makes one or two unambiguously peaceful gestures designed to reduce international tension. The theory predicts, and there is evidence to support the prediction (Etzioni, 1967; Pilisuk & Skolnik, 1968), that other parties, although they may be suspicious of the intent of these gestures, will test the waters by following suit. In this way a gradual increase in the intensity of peaceful gestures occurs. The theory spells out the steps that need to be taken.

1. Unilateral initiatives should be publicly announced before their execution.
2. Explicit invitations to reciprocate should be announced.
3. Initiatives should be continued over a considerable period of time, and they should be subject to verification by the other side.
4. Beginning initiatives should not reduce a nation's capacity to retaliate against an enemy. Initiatives should be graduated, with smaller concessions coming first.
5. The initiatives should be seen as voluntary.

Psychological Contributions to Peace

Perhaps nations are not like people; perhaps they do not have needs or motives. Their leaders do, however, and this places their behavior within the realm of psychology.

Because foreign affairs involve the perception by individuals of the motives, values, and attitudes of other individuals, much of what we know about social perception applies to international relations. We know that how we perceive others depends not only on their characteristics, but also upon our own. Furthermore, the context in which that perception occurs also influences our impressions. Our views of others are apt to be influenced by the views of those around us. In the realm of foreign relations, we are exposed almost exclusively to secondhand information about others. Relatively few Americans are personally acquainted with a Soviet citizen, yet nearly all Americans hold strong attitudes and beliefs about Russians. The extent to which these views are distorted is unknown, but we can be sure that in times of conflict misperception increases (White, 1985).

Otto Klineberg (1984) has noted psychology's contributions to the public debate over nuclear war and foreign affairs. These include many of the ideas reviewed above, such as Osgood's GRIT model and the conflict-resolution workshop developed by Kelman (Kelman & Cohen, 1976). In addition, psychologists have repeatedly found that bilateral communication, egalitarian personal contact, and joint cooperation on mutually beneficial tasks are effective ways to reduce misperception, stereotyping, and conflict.

Social Problem-Solving

How do we think about social problems and their solutions? What is the origin of our beliefs about such issues? Perhaps because of the way social problems are discussed in the press, presented to us by government officials, and studied by the scholars who are presumably expert in their nature, we are accustomed to thinking of them on a grand scale. Crime, child abuse, famine, and teenage suicide are conceived as national or global problems, by implication requiring national or global solutions. Perhaps a concerted effort by governments would eliminate human bloodshed and suffering. Hopes along such lines, however improbable they may be, are also ways of avoiding individual responsibility for action. The scale on which so many of us think about crime, for example, all but precludes attempting to do anything about it.

Varela (1970) has urged that social problems be considered on a local, even personal, level, a level at which one might be effective in bringing about change. While crime may flow from the top to the bottom of the social structure, its solution is not likely to do so. Because attitudes play a potent role in criminal violence, it is widespread attitude change that will be its undoing. And attitude change is most effective when it is immediate, a result of personal experience and face-to-face encounter.

References

Abel, G. G., Barlow, D. H., Blanchard, E., & Guild, D. (1977). The components of rapists' sexual arousal. *Archives of General Psychiatry, 34,* 895–903.

Abelson, R. P., Aronson, E., McGuire, W. J., Newcomb, T. M., Rosenberg, M. J., & Tannenbaum, P. H. (1968). *Theories of cognitive consistency: A sourcebook.* Chicago: Rand McNally.

Adams, D. B. (1984). Why there are so few women warriors. *Behavior Science Research, 18,* 1–13.

Alexander, J. F., & Parsons, B. V. (1973). Short-term behavioral intervention with delinquent families: Impact on family process and recidivism. *Journal of Abnormal Psychology, 81,* 219–225.

Alland, A., Jr. (1972). *The human imperative.* New York: Columbia University Press.

Allen, B. P. (1985). After the missiles: Sociopsychological effects of nuclear war. *American Psychologist, 40,* 927–937.

Amir, M. (1971). *Patterns in forcible rape.* Chicago: University of Chicago Press.

Anderson, C. A., & Anderson, D. C. (1984). Ambient temperature and violent crime: Tests of the linear and curvilinear hypotheses. *Journal of Personality and Social Psychology, 46,* 91–97.

Archer, D., & Gartner, R. (1984a). Homicide and the death penalty: A cross-national test of a deterrence hypothesis. In *Violence and crime in cross-national perspective.* New Haven: Yale University Press.

Archer, D., & Gartner, R. (1984b). *Violence and crime in cross-national perspective.* New Haven: Yale University Press.

Ardrey, R. (1961). *African genesis.* New York: Dell.

Ardrey, R. (1966). *The territorial imperative.* New York: Atheneum.

Arms, R. L., Russell, G. W., & Sandilands, M. L. (1979). Effects of viewing aggressive sports on the hostility of spectators. *Social Psychology Quarterly, 42,* 275–279.

Aronfreed, J. (1964). The origins of self-criticism. *Psychological Review, 71,* 193–218.

Aronfreed, J. (1968). *Conduct and conscience: The socialization of internalized control over behavior.* New York: Academic Press.

Aronson, E., Blaney, N., Sikes, J., Stephan, C., & Snapp, M. (1975). Busing and racial tension: The jigsaw route to learning and liking. *Psychology Today, 8,* 43–50.

Averill, J. R. (1982). *Anger and aggression: An essay on emotion.* New York: Springer-Verlag.

Averill, J. R. (1983). Studies on anger and aggression: Implications for theories of emotion. *American Psychologist, 38,* 1145–1160.

Bailey, W. C., & Smith, R. W. (1972). Punishment: Its severity and certainty. *Journal of Criminal Law, Criminology & Police Science, 63,* 530–539.

Bandura, A. (1965a). Influence of model's reinforcement contingencies on the acquisition of imitative responses. *Journal of Personality and Social Psychology, 1,* 589–595.

Bandura, A. (1965b). Vicarious processes. In L. Berkowitz (Ed.), *Advances in experimental social psychology.* New York: Academic Press.

Bandura, A. (1973). *Aggression: A social learning analysis.* Englewood Cliffs, NJ: Prentice-Hall.

Bandura, A. (1977). *Social learning theory.* Englewood Cliffs, NJ: Prentice-Hall.

Bandura, A., & Mischel, W. (1965). Modification of self-imposed delay of reward through exposure to live and symbolic models. *Journal of Personality and Social Psychology, 2,* 698–705.

Bandura, A., Ross, D., & Ross, S. A. (1963). Vicarious reinforcement and imitative learning. *Journal of Abnormal and Social Psychology, 67,* 601–607.

Bandura, A., Underwood, B., & Fromson, M. E. (1975). Disinhibition of aggression through diffusion of responsibility and dehumanization of victims. *Journal of Research in Personality, 9,* 253–269.

Barclay, A. M. (1971). Linking sexual and aggressive motives: Contributions of "irrelevant" arousals. *Journal of Personality, 39,* 481–492.

Barclay, A. M., & Haber, R. N. (1965). The relation of aggressive to sexual motivation. *Journal of Personality, 33,* 462–475.

Barlett, D. L., & Steele, J. B. (1973). Crime and injustice. *Philadelphia Inquirer.*

Barndt, R. J., & Johnson, D. M. (1955). Time orientation in delinquents. *Journal of Abnormal and Social Psychology, 51,* 343–345.

Barnett, S. A. (1983). Humanity and natural selection. *Ethology and Sociobiology, 4,* 35–51.

Baron, R. A. (1971). Reducing the influence of an aggressive model. *Journal of Personality and Social Psychology, 20,* 240–245.

Baron, R. A. (1974). The aggression-inhibiting influence of heightened sexual arousal. *Journal of Personality and Social Psychology, 30,* 318–322.

Baron, R. A. (1977). *Human aggression.* New York: Plenum.

Baron, R. A. (1979). Aggression and heat: The "long hot summer" revisited. In A. Baum, J. E. Singer & S. Valins (Eds.), *Advances in environmental psychology.* Hillsdale, NJ: Lawrence Erlbaum Associates.

Baron, R. A. (1983). The control of human aggression: A strategy based on incompatible responses. In R. G. Geen & E. Donnerstein (Eds.), *Aggression: Theoretical and empirical reviews.* New York: Academic Press.

Baron, R. A., & Ball, R. L. (1974). The aggression-inhibiting influence of nonhostile humor. *Journal of Experimental Social Psychology, 10,* 23–33.

Becker, H. S. (1953). Becoming a marijuana user. *American Journal of Sociology, 59,* 235–242.

Bem, D. J. (1966). Inducing belief in false confessions. *Journal of Personality and Social Psychology, 3,* 707–710.

Bennett, R. M., Buss, A. H., & Carpenter, J. A. (1969). Alcohol and human physical aggression. *Quarterly Journal of Studies on Alcohol, 30,* 870–876.

Berglas, S. (1985, February). Why did this happen to me? *Psychology Today, 19,* 44–48.

Berk, R. A., & Aldrich, H. E. (1972). Patterns of vandalism during civil disorders as an indicator of selection of targets. *American Sociological Review, 37,* 533–547.

Berkowitz, L. (1960). Repeated frustrations and expectations in hostility arousal. *Journal of Abnormal and Social Psychology, 60,* 422–429.

Berkowitz, L. (1962). *Aggression: A social psychological analysis.* New York: McGraw-Hill.

Berkowitz, L. (1965). Some aspects of observed aggression. *Journal of Personality and Social Psychology, 2,* 359–369.

Berkowitz, L. (1970a). Aggressive humor as a stimulus to aggressive responses. *Journal of Personality and Social Psychology, 16,* 710–717.

Berkowitz, L. (1970b). The contagion of violence: An S-R mediational analysis of some effects of observed violence. In W. J. Arnold & M. M. Page (Eds.), *Nebraska symposium on motivation.* Lincoln: University of Nebraska Press.

Berkowitz, L. (1970c). Experimental investigations of hostility catharsis. *Journal of Consulting & Clinical Psychology, 35,* 1–7.

Berkowitz, L. (1970d). The self, selfishness and altruism. In J. Macaulay & L. Berkowitz (Eds.), *Altruism and helping behavior.* New York: Academic Press.

Berkowitz, L. (1984). Some effects of thoughts on anti- and prosocial influences of media events: A cognitive-neoassociation analysis. *Psychological Bulletin, 95,* 410–427.

Berkowitz, L., & Alioto, J. T. (1973). The meaning of an observed event as a determinant of its aggressive consequences. *Journal of Personality and Social Psychology, 28,* 206–217.

Berkowitz, L., & Frodi, A. (1977). Stimulus characteristics that can enhance or decrease aggression: Associations with prior positive or negative reinforcements for aggression. *Aggressive Behavior, 3,* 1–15.

Berkowitz, L., & LePage, A. (1967). Weapons as aggression-eliciting stimuli. *Journal of Personality and Social Psychology, 7,* 202–207.

Berkowitz, L., & Macaulay, J. (1971). The contagion of criminal violence. *Sociometry, 34,* 328–360.

Binford, S. (1972). Apes and original sin. *Human Behavior, 1* (6), 64–71.

Bloch, H. A., & Geis, G. (1962). *Man, crime, and society.* New York: Random House.

Blumenthal. M. D., Kahn, R. L., Andrews, F. M., & Head, K. B. (1972). *Justifying violence: Attitudes of American men.* Ann Arbor, MI: Institute for Social Research.

Boring, E. G., Langfeld, H. S., & Weld, H. P. (1939). *Introduction to psychology.* New York: Wiley.

Bowers, W. J., & Pierce, G. L. (1980). Deterrence or brutalization:

What is the effect of executions? *Crime and Delinquency, 26,* 453–484.

Boyanowsky, E. O., Newtson, D., & Walster, E. (1974). Film preferences following a murder. *Communication Research, 1,* 32–43.

Bramel, D., Taub, B., & Blum, B. (1968). An observer's reaction to the suffering of his enemy. *Journal of Personality and Social Psychology, 8,* 384–392.

Brandt, A. (1984, July). Thinking about the end. *Esquire,* 25–26.

Brantingham, P. J., & Brantingham, P. L. (Eds.) (1981). *Environmental criminology.* Beverly Hills, CA: Sage.

Brier, S. S., & Fienberg, S. E. (1980). Recent econometric modeling of crime and punishment: Support for the deterrence hypothesis? In S. E. Fienberg & A. J. Reiss (Eds.), *Indicators of crime and criminal justice: Quantitative studies.* Washington, DC: U.S. Government Printing Office.

Brier, S., & Piliavin, I. M. (1965). Delinquency, situational determinants, and commitment to conformity. *Social Problems, 12,* 35–45.

Brock, T. C. (1968). Implications of commodity theory for value change. In A. G. Greenwald, T. C. Brock, & T. M. Ostrom (Eds.), *Psychological foundations of attitudes.* New York: Academic Press

Brock, T. C., & Buss, A. H. (1962). Dissonance, aggression, and evaluation of pain. *Journal of Abnormal and Social Psychology, 65,* 197–202.

Brock, T. C., & del Guidice, C. (1963). Stealing and temporal orientation. *Journal of Abnormal and Social Psychology, 66,* 91–94.

Bronfenbrenner, U. (1970). *Two worlds of childhood: U.S. and U.S.S.R.* New York: Russell Sage Foundation.

Brown, B. B., & Altman, I. (1981). Territoriality and residential crime: A conceptual framework. In P. J. Brantingham & P. L. Brantingham (Eds.), *Environmental criminology.* Beverly Hills, CA: Sage.

Bryan, J., & Test, M. A. (1967). Models and helping: Naturalistic studies in aiding behavior. *Journal of Personality and Social Psychology, 6,* 400–407.

Bryant, J., & Zillmann, D. (1983). Sports violence and the media. In J. H. Goldstein (Ed.), *Sports violence.* New York: Springer-Verlag.

Bureau of Justice Statistics. (1983). *Report to the Nation on Crime and Justice.* Washington, DC: U.S. Department of Justice.

Burgess, E. W. (1916). Juvenile delinquency in a small city. *Jour-*

nal of the American Institute of Criminal Law and Criminology. 6, 724–728.

Buss, A. H. (1963). Physical aggression in relation to different frustrations. *Journal of Abnormal and Social Psychology, 67,* 1–7.

Buss, A. H. (1971). Aggression pays. In J. L. Singer (Ed.), *The control of aggression and violence.* New York: Academic Press.

Buss, A. H., Booker, A., & Buss, E. (1972). Firing a weapon and aggression. *Journal of Personality and Social Psychology, 22,* 296–302.

Bynum, T. S., & Purri, D. M. (1984). Crime and architectural style: An examination of the environmental design hypothesis. *Criminal Justice and Behavior, 11,* 179–196.

Byrne, D. (1971). *The attraction paradigm.* New York: Academic Press.

Calhoun, J. B. (1962). Population density and social pathology. *Scientific American, 206,* 139–148.

Campbell, A. (1984). *Girls in the gang.* New York: Blackwell.

Campbell, D. T. (1969), Reforms as experiments. *American Psychologist, 24,* 409–429.

Campbell, J. S. (1970). Violence in America. In *New York Times Encyclopedic Almanac, 1971.* New York: New York Times.

Caprara, G. V., Renzi, P., Amolini, P., & Dimperio, G. (1984). The eliciting cue value of aggressive slides reconsidered in a personological perspective: The weapons effect and irritability. *European Journal of Social Psychology, 14,* 313–322.

Carmen, Rieker, & Mills. (February, 1985). *Psychology Today.*

Carroll, J. C. (1977). The intergenerational transmission of family violence: The long-term effects of aggressive behavior. *Aggressive Behavior, 3,* 289–299.

Carver, C. S., & Glass, D. C. (1977). The coronary prone behavior pattern and interpersonal aggression. Unpublished ms. University of Texas.

Caughey, J. L. (1984). *Imaginary social worlds.* Lincoln: University of Nebraska Press.

Chaffee, S., & McLeod, J. (1971). Adolescents, parents, and television violence. Paper presented at American Psychological Association. Washington, DC.

Chambliss, W. J. (1966). The deterrent influence of punishment. *Crime & Delinquency, 12,* 70–75.

Chandler, M. J. (1973). Egocentrism and antisocial behavior: The assessment and training of social perspective-taking skills. *Developmental Psychology, 9,* 326–332.

Chorover, S. (1979). *From genesis to genocide*. Cambridge, MA: MIT Press.

Clark, D. G., & Blankenburg, W. B. (1972). Trends in violent content in selected mass media. In G. A. Comstock & E. A. Rubinstein (Eds.), *Television and social behavior*. Vol. 1. Washington, DC: U.S. Government Printing Office.

Clark, K. B. (1971). The pathos of power. *American Psychologist, 26,* 1047–1057.

Clark, R. (1970). *Crime in America*. New York: Simon & Schuster.

Cline, V. B., Croft, R. G., & Courrier, S. (1973). Desensitization of children to television violence. *Journal of Personality and Social Psychology, 27,* 360–365.

Cohn, E. S., Kidder, L. H., & Harvey, J. (1978). Crime prevention vs. crime victimization prevention: The psychology of two different reactions. *Victimology, 3,* 285–296.

Comstock, G., Chaffee, S., Katzman, N., McCombs, M., & Roberts, D. (1978). *Television in America*. Beverly Hills, CA: Sage.

Cordes, C. (1984, November). Findings debunk aggression as evolutionary inheritance. *APA Monitor*.

Cousins, N. (1971). *Anatomy of an illness*. New York: Norton.

Critchlow, B. (1983). Blaming the booze: The attribution of responsibility for drunken behavior. *Personality and Social Psychology Bulletin, 9,* 451–473.

David, P., & Scott, J. (1973). A cross-cultural comparison of juvenile offenders, offenses, due process, and societies. *Criminology, 11,* 183–205.

Davis, D., Rainey, H., & Brock, T. C. (1976). Interpersonal physical pleasuring: Effects of sex combinations, recipient attributes, and anticipated future interaction. *Journal of Personality and Social Psychology, 33,* 89–106.

Decker, J. F. (1972). Curbside deterrence? An analysis of the effect of a slug-rejector device, coin-view window, and warning labels on slug usage in New York City parking meters. *Criminology, 10,* 127–142.

Delgado, J. M. R. (1967). Aggression and defense under cerebral radio control. In C. D. Clemente & D. B. Lindsley (Eds.), *Aggression and defense: Neural mechanisms and social patterns*. Los Angeles: University of California Press.

Delgado, J. M. R. (1969). *Physical control of the mind*. New York: Harper & Row.

Dengerink, H. A. (1971). Aggression, anxiety, and physiological arousal. *Journal of Experimental Research in Personality, 5,* 223–232.

Diamond, B. (1974). The psychiatric prediction of dangerousness. *University of Pennsylvania Law Review, 123,* 439–452.

Diener, E. (1976). Effects of prior destructive behavior, anonymity, and group presence on deindividuation and aggression. *Journal of Personality and Social Psychology, 33,* 497–507.

Diener, E. (1977). Deindividuation: Causes and consequences. *Social Behavior and Personality, 5,* 143–155.

Dobash, R. E., & Dobash, R. P. (1984). The nature and antecedents of violent events. *British Journal of Criminology, 24,* 269–288.

Dollard, J., Doob, L. W., Miller, N. E., Mowrer, O. H., & Sears, R. R. (1939). *Frustration and aggression.* New Haven: Yale University Press.

Dorfman, A. (1984, October). The criminal mind. *Science Digest, 92,* 44–47, 98.

Dworkin, E. S., & Efran, J. S. (1967). The angered: Their susceptibility to varieties of humor. *Journal of Personality and Social Psychology, 6,* 233–236.

Edelman, E. M., & Goldstein, A. P. (1981). Moral education. In A. P. Goldstein, E. G. Carr, W S. Davidson, & P. Wehr (Eds.), *In response to aggression.* New York: Pergamon.

Ehrlich, I. (1975). The deterrent effect of capital punishment: A question of life and death. *American Economic Review, 65,* 397–417.

Ellis, G. T., & Sekyra, F. (1972). The effect of aggressive cartoons on the behavior of first grade children. *Journal of Psychology, 81,* 37–43.

Emshoff, J. G., Davis, D. D., & Davidson, W. S. (1981). Social support and aggression. In A. P. Goldstein, E. G. Carr, W. S. Davidson, & P. Wehr (Eds.), *In response to aggression.* New York: Pergamon.

Endler, N. S., & Hunt, J. McV. (1968). S-R inventories of hostility and comparisons of the proportions of variance from persons, responses, and situations for hostility and anxiousness. *Journal of Personality and Social Psychology, 9,* 309–315.

Erlanger, H. S. (1976). Is there a "subculture of violence" in the south? *Journal of Criminal Law and Criminology, 66,* 483–490.

Eron, L. D., & Huesmann, L. R. (1984). The control of aggressive behavior by changes in attitudes, values, and the conditions of learning. In R. J. Blanchard & D. C. Blanchard (Eds.), *Advances in the study of aggression.* Vol. 1. Orlando, FL: Academic Press.

Eron, L. D., Huesmann, L. R., Lefkowitz, M. M., & Walder, L. O.

(1972). Does television violence cause aggression? *American Psychologist, 27,* 253–263.

Etzioni, A. (1967). The Kennedy experiment. *Western Political Quarterly, 20,* 361–380.

Farber, M. L. (1955). Psychoanalytic hypotheses in the study of war. *Journal of Social Issues, 11,* 29–35.

Farley, F., & Farley, S. (1972). Stimulus-seeking motivation and delinquent behavior among institutionalized delinquent girls. *Journal of Consulting and Clinical Psychology, 39,* 94–97.

Farrington, D. P. (1983). Offending from 10 to 25 years of age. In K. T. van Dusen & S. A. Mednick (Eds.), *Prospective studies of crime and delinquency.* Boston: Kluwer-Nijhoff.

Feierabend, I. K., & Feierabend, R. L. (1966). Aggressive behavior within polities, 1948–1962: A cross-national study. *Journal of Conflict Resolution, 10,* 249–271.

Feierabend, I. K., and Feierabend, R. L. (1972). Systemic conditions of political aggression: An application of frustration-aggression theory. In I. K. Feierabend, R. L. Feierabend, & T. R. Gurr (Eds.), *Anger, violence, and politics.* Englewood Cliffs, NJ: Prentice-Hall.

Feierabend, I. K., Feierabend, R. L., & Scanland, F. (1972). The relation between sources of systemic frustration, international conflict, and political instability. In I. K. Feierabend, R. L. Feierabend, & T. R. Gurr (Eds.), *Anger, violence, and politics.* Englewood Cliffs, NJ: Prentice-Hall.

Feindler, E. L., Marriott, S. A., & Iwata, M. (1984). Group anger control training for junior high school delinquents. *Cognitive Therapy and Research, 8,* 299–311.

Felson, R. B. (1982). Impression management and the escalation of aggression and violence. *Social Psychology Quarterly, 45,* 245–254.

Felson, R. B., Ribner, S. A., & Siegel, M. S. (1984). Age and the effect of third parties during criminal violence. *Sociology & Social Research, 68,* 452–462.

Feshbach, N. D., & Feshbach, S. (1969). The relationship between empathy and aggression in two age groups. *Developmental Psychology, 1,* 102–107.

Feshbach, S. Aggression. (1970). In P. H. Mussen (Ed.), *Carmichael's manual of child psychology.* Vol. 2. New York: Wiley.

Feshbach, S. (1980). Interview, in J. H. Goldstein, *Social psychology.* New York: Academic Press.

Feshbach, S., & Singer, R. D. (1971). *Television and aggression.* San Francisco: Jossey-Bass.

Festinger, L. (1954). Theory of social comparison processes. *Human Relations, 7,* 117–140.

Festinger, L. (1957). *A theory of cognitive dissonance.* Stanford: Stanford University Press.

Fine, G. A. (1983). Sociological approaches to the study of humor. In P. E. McGhee & J. H. Goldstein (Eds.), *Handbook of humor research.* Vol. 1. *Basic issues.* New York: Springer-Verlag.

Fishkin, J., Keniston, K., & MacKinnon, C. (1973). Moral reasoning and political ideology. *Journal of Personality and Social Psychology, 27,* 109–119.

Flynn, J. P. (1967). The neural basis of aggression in cats. In D. C. Glass (Ed.), *Neurophysiology and emotion.* New York: Rockefeller University Press.

Freedman, J. L. (1975). *Crowding and behavior.* San Francisco: Freeman.

Freedman, J. L. (1984). Effect of television violence on aggressiveness. *Psychological Bulletin, 96,* 227–246.

Freedman, J. L., & Fraser, S. C. (1966). Compliance without pressure: The foot-in-the-door technique. *Journal of Personality and Social Psychology, 4,* 195–202.

Freedman, J. L., Klevansky, S., & Ehrlich, P. R. (1971). The effect of crowding on human task performance. *Journal of Applied Social Psychology, 1,* 7–25.

Freedman, J. L., Levy, A., Buchanan, R. W., & Price, J. (1972). Crowding and human aggressiveness. *Journal of Experimental Social Psychology, 8,* 528–548.

Freud, S. (1960). *Jokes and their relation to the unconscious.* (J. Strachey, Trans.) New York: Norton. (Original work published 1905)

Freud, S. (1955). Beyond the pleasure principle. Vol. 18. Civilization and its discontents. Vol. 21. J. Strachey (Ed.), *The standard edition of the complete psychological works of Sigmund Freud.* London: Hogarth. (Original work published 1930)

Freud, S., & Einstein, A. (1934). *Why war?* London: Hogarth.

Frodi, A. (1977). Sexual arousal, situational restrictiveness, and aggressive behavior. *Journal of Research in Personality, 11,* 48–58.

Frodi, A., Macaulay, J., & Thome, P. R. (1977). Are women always less aggressive than men? A review of the experimental literature. *Psychological Bulletin, 84,* 634–660.

Fromkin, H. L., & Brock, T. C. (1973). Erotic materials: A commodity theory analysis of the enhanced desirability that may accompany their unavailability. *Journal of Applied Social Psychology, 3,* 219–231.

Fromkin, H. L., Goldstein, J. H., & Brock, T. C. (1977). The role of "irrelevant" derogation in hostility catharsis: A field experiment. *Journal of Experimental Social Psychology, 13,* 239–252.

Gastil, R. D. (1971). Homicide and a regional culture of violence. *American Sociological Review, 36,* 412–427.

Geen, R. G., & O'Neal, E. C. (1969). Activation of cue-elicited aggression by general arousal. *Journal of Personality and Social Psychology, 11,* 289–292.

Geen, R. G., & Pigg, R. R. (1970). Acquisition of an aggressive response and its generalization to verbal behavior. *Journal of Personality and Social Psychology, 15,* 165–170.

Gelles, R. J. (1980). A profile of violence toward children in the United States. In G. Gerbner, C. J. Ross, & E. Zigler (Eds.), *Child abuse: An agenda for action.* New York: Oxford University Press.

Gelles, R. J., & Straus, M. A. (1979). Determinants of violence in the family: Toward a theoretical integration. In W. R. Burr, R. Hill, F. I. Nye, & I. L. Reiss (Eds.), *Contemporary theories about the family.* New York: Free Press.

Gergen, K. J., Ellsworth, P., Maslach, C., & Seipel, M. (1975). Obligations, donor resources, and reactions to aid in three cultures. *Journal of Personality and Social Psychology, 31,* 390–400.

Gergen, K. J., Morse, S. J., & Kristeller, J. L. (1973). The manner of giving: Cross-national continuities in reactions to aid. *Psychologia, 16,* 121–131.

Gill, D. (1970). *Violence against children.* Cambridge, MA: Harvard University Press.

Glover, E. (1960). *The roots of crime.* New York: International Universities Press.

Goldstein, A. P., & Rosenbaum, A. (1982). *Aggress-less: How to turn anger and aggression into positive action.* Englewood Cliffs, NJ: Prentice-Hall.

Goldstein, J. H. (1972). Preference for aggressive movie content: The effects of cognitive salience. Unpublished ms. Temple University.

Goldstein, J. H. (1976). Theoretical notes on humor. *Journal of Communication, 26* (3), 102–112.

Goldstein, J. H. (1980). Micro- and macro-escalation of human aggression. Paper presented at Eastern Psychological Association. Hartford, CT.

Goldstein, J. H. (1981). On political assassination and heinous crimes. *Aggressive Behavior, 7,* 268–270.

Goldstein, J. H. (1982a). Sports violence. *National Forum, 62,* 9–11.

Goldstein, J. H. (1982b, August/September). A laugh a day: Can mirth keep disease at bay? *The Sciences, 22,* 21–25.

Goldstein, J. H. (1983). Introduction. *Sports violence.* New York: Springer-Verlag.

Goldstein, J. H. (1985a). I fattori temporali della condotta aggressiva: L'effetto 'escalation.' In G. V. Caprara & P. Renzi (Eds.), *L'Aggressività Umana.* Rome: Bulzoni.

Goldstein, J. H. (1985b). Athletic performance and spectator behavior: The humanistic concerns of sports psychology. In W. L. Umphlett (Ed.), *American sport culture: The humanistic dimension.* Lewisburg, PA: Bucknell University Press.

Goldstein, J. H. (1986a). *Reporting science: The case of aggression.* Hillsdale, NJ: Lawrence Erlbaum Associates.

Goldstein, J. H. (1986b). Social science, journalism, and public policy. In J. H. Goldstein (Ed.), *Reporting science: The case of aggression.* Hillsdale, NJ: Lawrence Erlbaum Associates.

Goldstein, J. H., & Arms, R. L. (1971). Effects of observing athletic contests on hostility. *Sociometry, 34,* 83–90.

Goldstein, J. H., & Bredemeier, B. J. (1977). Sport and socialization: Some basic issues. *Journal of Communication, 27,* 154–159.

Goldstein, J. H., Davis, R. W., & Herman, D. (1975). Escalation of aggression: Experimental studies. *Journal of Personality and Social Psychology, 31,* 162–170.

Goldstein, J. H., Davis, R. W., Kernis, M., & Cohn, E. S. (1981). Retarding the escalation of aggression. *Social Behavior and Personality, 9,* 65–70.

Goldstein, J. H., Rosnow, R. L., Raday, T., Silverman, I., & Gaskell, G. D. (1975). Punitiveness in response to films varying in content: A cross-national field study of aggression. *European Journal of Social Psychology, 5,* 149–165.

Goldstein, J. H., Suls, J. M., & Anthony, S. (1972). Enjoyment of specific types of humor content: Motivation or salience? In J. H. Goldstein & P. E. McGhee (Eds.), *The psychology of humor.* New York: Academic Press.

Goode, W. (1969). Violence among intimates. In D. J. Mulvihill & M. M. Tumin (Eds.), *Crimes of violence.* Washington, DC: U.S. Government Printing Office.

Graham, S., Doubleday, C., & Guarino, P. A. (1984). The development of the relations between perceived controllability and the emotions of pity, anger, and guilt. *Child Development, 55,* 561–565.

Green, M. R. (Ed.). (1980). *Violence and the family.* Boulder, CO: Westview Press.

Grotjahn, M. (1957). *Beyond laughter.* New York: McGraw-Hill.

Guzé, S. (1976). *Criminality and psychiatric disorders.* New York: Oxford University Press.

Hammond, M. (1984). Contributions of evolutionary perspective to peace. Paper presented at American Psychological Association. Toronto.

Haney, C., Banks, C., & Zimbardo, P. (1973). Interpersonal dynamics in a simulated prison. *International Journal of Criminology & Penology, 1,* 69–97.

Hanson, C. L., Henggeler, S. W., Haefele, W. F., & Rodick, J. D. (1984). Demographic, individual, and family relationship correlates of serious and repeated crime among adolescents and their siblings. *Journal of Consulting and Clinical Psychology, 52,* 528–538.

Harrell, W. A. (1981). Verbal aggressiveness in spectators at professional hockey games: The effects of tolerance of violence and amount of exposure to hockey. *Human Relations, 34,* 643–655.

Hawkins, R. P., Peterson, R. F., Schweid, E., & Bijou, S. W. (1966). Behavior therapy in the home: Amelioration of problem parent-child relations with the parent in a therapeutic role. *Journal of Experimental Child Psychology, 4,* 99–107.

Heath, R. G. (1963). Electrical self-stimulation of the brain in man. *American Journal of Psychiatry, 120,* 571–577.

Hennigan, K. M., Del Rosario, M. L., Heath, L., Cook, T. D., Wharton, J. D., & Calder, B. J. (1982). Impact of the introduction of television on crime in the United States: Empirical findings and theoretical implications. *Journal of Personality and Social Psychology, 42,* 461–477.

Henry, A. F., & Short, J. F., Jr. (1954). *Suicide and homicide.* New York: Free Press.

Herrenkohl, R. C., Herrenkohl, E. C., & Egolf, C. P. (1983). Circumstances surrounding the occurrence of child maltreatment. *Journal of Consulting and Clinical Psychology, 51,* 424–431.

Hirschi, T., & Hindelang, M. J. (1977). Intelligence and delinquency: A revisionist review. *American Sociological Review, 42,* 571–587.

Hoffman, M. L. (1970). Moral development. In P. H. Mussen (Ed.), *Carmichael's manual of child psychology.* Vol. 2. New York: Wiley.

Hokanson, J. E. (1970). Psychophysiological evaluation of the catharsis hypothesis. In E. I. Megargee & J. E. Hokanson (Eds.), *The dynamics of aggression*. New York: Harper & Row.

Holland, T. R., Beckett, G. E., & Levi, M. (1981). Intelligence, personality, and criminal violence: A multivariate analysis. *Journal of Consulting and Clinical Psychology, 49*, 106–111.

Holper, L. J., Goldstein, J. H., & Snyderman, P. (1974). The placement of neutral stimulus material in reducing the impact of aggression in the mass media. *Representative Research in Social Psychology, 4*, 28–35.

Hooton, E. A. (1937). *Apes, men, and morons*. New York: Putnam.

Hornstein, H. A. (1973). Promotive tension: The basis of prosocial behavior from a Lewinian perspective. In L. G. Wispe (Ed.), *Positive forms of social behavior. Journal of Social Issues, 28* (3), 191–218.

Hovland, C. I., & Sears, R. R. (1940). Minor studies of aggression. VI. Correlations of lynchings with economic indices. *Journal of Psychology, 9*, 301–310.

Hudgins, W., & Prentice, N. M. (1973). Moral judgment in delinquent and nondelinquent adolescents and their mothers. *Journal of Abnormal Psychology, 82*, 145–152.

Huesmann, L. R., Eron, L. D., Klein, R., Brice, P., & Fischer, P. (1983). Mitigating the imitation of aggressive behaviors by changing children's attitudes about media violence. *Journal of Personality and Social Psychology, 44*, 899–910.

Huppes, T. (1976). Anomie and inflation. In T. Huppes (Ed.), *Economics and sociology: Towards an integration*. Leiden, Netherlands: Martinus Nijhoff.

Hyde, J. S. (1984). How large are gender differences in aggression? A developmental meta-analysis. *Developmental Psychology, 20*, 722–736.

Isen, A. M. (1970). Success, failure, attention and reaction to others: The warm glow of success. *Journal of Personality and Social Psychology, 15*, 294–301.

Isen, A. M., & Levin, P. F. (1972). Effect of feeling good on helping: Cookies and kindness. *Journal of Personality and Social Psychology, 21*, 384–388.

Ittelson, W., & Proshansky, H. (1972). *Environmental psychology*. New York: Holt, Rinehart and Winston.

Jacobs, P., Brunton, M., & Melville, M. (1965). Aggressive behavior, mental sub-normality, and the XYY male. *Nature, 208*, 1351–1352.

Jaffe, Y., Shapir, N., & Yinon, Y. (1981). Aggression and its escalation. *Journal of Cross-Cultural Psychology, 12,* 21–36.

Jahoda, G., & Harrison, S. (1975). Belfast children: Some effects of a conflict environment. *Irish Journal of Psychology, 1,* 1–19.

James, W. (1911). The moral equivalent of war. *Memoirs and studies.* London: Longmans.

Janis, I. L. (1971). Groupthink among policy makers. In N. Sanford & C. Comstock (Eds.), *Sanctions for evil.* San Francisco: Jossey-Bass.

Jarvik, L. F., Klodin, V., & Matsuyama, S. S. (1973). Human aggression and the extra Y chromosome. *American Psychologist, 28,* 674–682.

Jeffery, C. R. (1971). *Crime prevention through environmental design* (2nd ed., 1977). Beverly Hills, CA: Sage.

Johnson, N. (1967). *How to talk back to your television set.* Boston: Little, Brown.

Jones, C., & Aronson, E. (1973). Attribution of fault to a rape victim as a function of respectability of the victim. *Journal of Personality and Social Psychology, 26,* 415–419.

Kagan, J., & Moss. H. A. (1962). *Birth to maturity: A study in psychological development.* New York: Wiley.

Kaufmann, H. (1970). *Aggression and altruism.* New York: Holt, Rinehart and Winston.

Keefer, R., Goldstein, J. H., & Kasiarz, D. (1983). Olympic Games participation and warfare. In J. H. Goldstein (Ed.), *Sports violence.* New York: Springer-Verlag.

Kelman, H. C., & Cohen, S. P. (1976). The problem-solving workshop: A social psychological contribution to the resolution of international conflicts. *Journal of Peace Research, 13,* 79–90.

Kelman, H. C., & Lawrence, L. H. (1972). Assignment of responsibility in the case of Lt. Calley: Preliminary report on a national survey. *Journal of Social Issues, 28,* 177–212.

Kercher, G. A., & Walker, C. E. (1973). Reactions of convicted rapists to sexually explicit stimuli. *Journal of Abnormal Psychology, 81,* 46–50.

Kevles, D. J. (1985). *In the name of eugenics.* New York: Knopf.

Kim, S. S. (1976). The Lorenzian theory of aggression and peace research: A critique. *Journal of Peace Research, 13,* 253–276.

Kipnis, D. (1968). Studies in character structure. *Journal of Personality and Social Psychology, 8,* 217–227.

Kipnis, D., Castell, P. J., Gergen, M., & Mauch, D. (1976). Metamorphic effects of power. *Journal of Applied Psychology, 61,* 127–135.

Klineberg, O. (1964). *The human dimension in international relations*. New York: Holt, Rinehart and Winston.

Klineberg, O. (1984). Public opinion and nuclear war. *American Psychologist, 39,* 1245–1253.

Klockars, C. B. (1985). *The idea of police*. Beverly Hills, CA: Sage.

Kniveton, B. H. (1973). The effect of rehearsal delay on long-term imitation of filmed aggression. *British Journal of Psychology, 64,* 259–265.

Knott, P. D., Lasater, L., & Shuman, R. (1974). Aggression-guilt and conditionability for aggressiveness. *Journal of Personality, 42,* 332–344.

Kohlberg, L. (1963). Moral development and identification. In H. W. Stevenson (Ed.), *Child psychology: 62nd yearbook of the National Society for the Study of Education*. Chicago: University of Chicago Press.

Kohlberg, L. (1976). Moral stages and moralization: The cognitive-developmental approach. In T. Lickona (Ed.), *Moral development and behavior*. New York: Holt, Rinehart and Winston.

Kohlberg, L., Scharf, P., & Hickey, J. (1972). The justice structure of the prison: A theory and an intervention. *Prison Journal, 51,* 3–14.

Kohlberg, L., & Turiel, E. (1971). Moral development and moral education. In G. S. Lesser (Ed.), *Psychology and educational practice*. Chicago: Scott, Foresman.

Konečni, V. J. (1975). Annoyance, type and duration of postannoyance activity, and aggression: The "cathartic effect." *Journal of Experimental Psychology: General, 104,* 76–102.

Konečni, V. J., and Ebbesen, E. B. (1976). Disinhibition versus the cathartic effect: Artifact and substance. *Journal of Personality and Social Psychology, 34,* 352–365.

Kreutzer, J. S., Schneider, H. G., & Myatt, C. R. (1984). Alcohol, aggression and assertiveness in men: Dosage and expectancy effects. *Journal of Studies on Alcohol, 45,* 275–278.

Krystal, H. (1982). The psychoanalytic (self-conscious) approach to aggression. In B. L. Danto, J. Bruhns, & A. H. Kutscher (Eds.), *The human side of homicide*. New York: Columbia University Press.

Kuhlman, T. L. (1985). A study of salience and motivational theories of humor. *Journal of Personality and Social Psychology, 49,* 281–286.

Landau, S. F. (1984). Trends in violence and aggression: A cross-cultural analysis. *International Journal of Comparative Sociology, 25,* 133–158.

Landau, S. F., & Beit-Hallahmi, B. (1983). Aggression in Israel: A psychohistorical perspective. In A. P. Goldstein & M. Segall (Eds.), *Aggression in global perspective.* New York: Pergamon.

Larsen, K. S., Coleman, D., Forbes, J., & Johnson, R. (1972). Is the subject's personality or the experimental situation a better predictor of a subject's willingness to administer shock to a victim? *Journal of Personality and Social Psychology, 22,* 287–295.

Latané, B., & Darley, J. (1970). *The unresponsive bystander: Why doesn't he help?* New York: Appleton-Century-Crofts.

Lazarus, R. S., Coyne, J. C., & Folkman, S. (1982). Cognition, emotion, and motivation: The doctoring of Humpty Dumpty. In R. W. J. Neufeld (Ed.). *Psychological stress and psychopathology.* New York: McGraw-Hill.

Lerner, M. J. (1970). The desire for justice and reactions to victims. In J. Macaulay & L. Berkowitz (Eds.), *Altruism and helping behavior.* New York: Academic Press.

Lerner, M. J. (1980). *The belief in a just world.* New York: Plenum.

Lessard, S. (1971, June). Busting our mental blocks on drugs and crime. *Washington Monthly, 3,* 6–18.

Lever, J. (1969). Soccer: Opium of the Brazilian people. *Transaction, 7* (2), 36–43.

Lewontin, R. C., Rose, S., & Kamin, L. J. (1984). *Not in our genes: Biology, ideology, and human nature.* New York: Pantheon.

Leyens, J.-P., & Parke, R. E. (1975). Aggressive slides can induce a weapons effect. *European Journal of Social Psychology, 5,* 229–236.

Loew, C. A. (1967). Acquisition of a hostile attitude and its relation to aggressive behavior. *Journal of Personality and Social Psychology, 5,* 552–558.

Lofton, C. (1980). Alternative estimates of the impact of certainty and severity of punishment on levels of homicide in American states. In S. E. Fienberg & A. J. Reiss (Eds.), *Indicators of crime and criminal justice: Quantitative studies.* Washington, DC: U.S. Government Printing Office.

London, P. (1970). The rescuers: Motivational hypotheses about Christians who saved Jews from the Nazis. In J. Macaulay & L. Berkowitz (Eds.), *Altruism and helping behavior.* New York: Academic Press.

Lorenz, K. (1964). Ritualized fighting. In J. D. Carthy & E. J. Ebling (Eds.), *The natural history of aggression.* New York: Academic Press.

Lorenz, K. (1966). *On aggression.* New York: Harcourt Brace World.

LoSciuto, L. A. (1972). A national inventory of television viewing behavior. In E. A. Rubinstein, G. A. Comstock, & J. P. Murray (Eds.), *Television and social behavior*. Vol. 4. Washington, DC: U.S. Government Printing Office.

Louscher, P. K., Hosford, R. E., & Moss, C. S. (1983). Predicting dangerous behavior in a penitentiary using the Megargee typology. *Criminal Justice and Behavior, 10,* 269–284.

Lumsden, C. J., & Wilson, E. O. (1981). *The coevolutionary process*. Cambridge, MA: Harvard University Press.

Lyle, J., & Hoffman, H. R. (1972). Children's use of television and other media. In E. A. Rubinstein, G. A. Comstock, & J. P. Murray (Eds.), *Television and social behavior*. Vol. 4. Washington, DC: U.S. Government Printing Office.

Maccoby, E. E. (1968). The development of moral values and behavior in childhood. In J. A. Clausen (Ed.), *Socialization and society*. Boston: Little, Brown.

MacDonald, J. M. (1961). *The murderer and his victim*. Springfield, IL: Chas. C. Thomas.

Malamuth, N. M., Check, J., & Briere, J. Sexual arousal to aggression: Ideological, aggressive, and sexual correlates. *Journal of Personality and Social Psychology,* in press.

Malamuth, N. M., & Donnerstein, E. (Eds.), (1984). *Pornography and sexual aggression*. Orlando, FL: Academic Press.

Mann, L. (1973). Attitudes toward My Lai and obedience to orders: An Australian survey. *Australian Journal of Psychology, 25,* 11–21.

Mann, L. (1979). Sports crowds from the perspective of collective behavior. In J. H. Goldstein (Ed.), *Sports, games, and play*. Hillsdale, NJ: Lawrence Erlbaum Associates.

Mark, V. H., & Ervin, F. R. (1970). *Violence and the brain*. New York: Harper & Row.

Markham, J. M. (1973, March). Heroin hunger does not a mugger make. *New York Times Magazine*.

Marlatt, G. A., Kosturn, C., & Lang, A. (1975). Provocation to anger and opportunity for retaliation as determinants of alcohol consumption in social drinkers. *Journal of Abnormal Psychology, 84,* 652–659.

Marlatt, G. A., & Rohsenow, D. J. (1981, December). The think-drink effect. *Psychology Today,* 60–69, 93.

Marohn, R. C., Offer, D., & Ostrov, E. (1971). Juvenile delinquents view their impulsivity. *American Journal of Psychiatry, 128,* 418–423.

May, R. (1972). *Power and innocence: A search for the source of violence*. New York: Norton.

McCauley, C., Woods, K., Coolidge, C., & Kulick, W. (1983). More aggressive cartoons are funnier. *Journal of Personality and Social Psychology, 44,* 817–823.

McCord, J. (1983). A longitudinal study of aggression and antisocial behavior. In K. T. van Dusen & S. A. Mednick (Eds.), *Prospective studies of crime and delinquency.* Boston: Kluwer-Nijhoff.

McCord, W., McCord, J., & Zola, L. K. (1959). *Origins of crime: A new evaluation of the Cambridge-Somerville youth study.* New York: Columbia University Press.

McGurk, B. J. (1978). Personality types among "normal" homicides. *British Journal of Criminology, 18,* 146–161.

McPhee, J. (1984). *La Place de la Concorde Suisse.* New York: Farrar, Straus & Giroux.

Megargee, E. I. (1966). Undercontrolled and overcontrolled personality types in extreme antisocial aggression. *Psychological Monographs, 80* (3).

Megargee, E. I. (1972). *The psychology of violence and aggression.* Morristown, NJ: General Learning Press.

Megargee, E. I., Cook, P. E., & Mendelsohn, G. A. (1967). Development and evaluation of an MMPI scale of assaultiveness in overcontrolled individuals. *Journal of Abnormal Psychology, 72,* 519–528.

Menninger, K. (1968). *The crime of punishment.* New York: Viking.

Merton, R. K. (1957). *Social theory and social structure.* Glencoe, IL: Free Press.

Merton, R. K., & Kitt, A. S. (1952). Contributions to the theory of reference group behavior. In R. K. Merton & P. F. Lazarsfeld (Eds.), *Studies in the scope and method of 'The American soldier.'* New York: Free Press.

Messner, S. F. (1980). Income inequality and murder rates: Some cross-national findings. In R. F. Tomasson (Ed.), *Comparative social research.* Vol. 3. Greenwich, CT: JAI Press.

Milgram, S. (1974). *Obedience to authority.* New York: Harper & Row.

Milgram, S., & Shotland, R. L. (1973). *Television and antisocial behavior.* New York: Academic Press.

Mischel, W. (1971). *Introduction to personality.* New York: Holt, Rinehart and Winston.

Mischel, W., & Staub, E. (1965). Effects of expectancy on working and waiting for larger rewards. *Journal of Personality and Social Psychology, 2,* 625–633.

Mitford, J. (1973). *Kind and usual punishment.* New York: Knopf.

Monahan, J. (1980). *The clinical prediction of violent behavior.* Washington, DC: U.S. Government Printing Office.

Monahan, J. (1983). *Predicting violent behavior.* Beverly Hills, CA: Sage.

Montagu, A. (Ed.). (1968). *Man and aggression.* New York: Oxford University Press.

Montagu, A. (1976). *The nature of human aggression.* New York: Oxford University Press.

Montagu, A. (Ed.). (1978). *Learning non-aggression: The experience of non-literate societies.* New York: Oxford University Press.

Morawski, J., & Goldstein, S. (1985). Psychology and nuclear war: A chapter in our legacy of social responsibility. *American Psychologist, 40,* 276–284.

Morris, D. (1967). *The naked ape.* New York: McGraw-Hill.

Morris, N., & Hawkins, G. (1970). *The honest politician's guide to crime control.* Chicago: University of Chicago Press.

Moss, C. S., Johnson, M. E., & Hosford, R. E. (1984). An assessment of the Megargee typology in lifelong criminal violence. *Criminal Justice and Behavior, 11,* 225–234.

Moyer, K. E. (1968). Kinds of aggression and their physiological bases. *Communications in Behavioral Biology, 2* (a), 65–87.

Moyer, K. E. (1971a). Brain research must contribute to world peace. In K. E. Moyer (Ed.), *The physiology of hostility.* Chicago: Markham.

Moyer, K. E. (1971b). *The physiology of hostility.* Chicago: Markham.

Moyer, K. E. (1976). *The psychobiology of aggression.* New York: Harper & Row.

Mummendey, A. (1984). *The social psychology of aggression.* Heidelberg: Springer-Verlag.

Murphy, L. B. (1937). *Social behavior and child personality: An exploratory study of some roots of sympathy.* New York: Columbia University Press.

Mussen, P. H., & Rutherford, E. (1961). Effects of aggressive cartoons on children's aggressive play. *Journal of Abnormal and Social Psychology, 62,* 461–464.

Myrdal, G. (1944). *An American dilemma.* New York: Harper.

Nader, R. (1985, May). America's crime without criminals: White-collar fraud. *New York Times.*

National Advisory Commission on Civil Disorders. (1968). *Report to the National Advisory Commission on Civil Disorders.* New York: Bantam.

National Commission on the Causes and Prevention of Violence. (1968). *To establish justice, to insure domestic tranquility.* Washington, DC: U.S. Government Printing Office.

National Council on Crime and Delinquency. (1973). The nondangerous offender should not be imprisoned: A policy statement. *Crime & Delinquency, 19,* 449–456.

National Institute of Mental Health. (1982). *Television and behavior: Ten years of scientific progress and implications for the eighties.* Washington, DC: U.S. Government Printing Office.

Nevo, O., & Nevo, B. (1983). What do you do when asked to answer humorously? *Journal of Personality and Social Psychology, 44,* 188–193.

Newman, O. (1972). *Defensible space.* New York: Macmillan.

Obrdlik, A. J. (1942). Gallows humor: A sociological phenomenon. *American Journal of Sociology, 47,* 709–716.

Olweus, D. (1979). Stability of aggressive reaction patterns in males: A review. *Psychological Bulletin, 86,* 852–875.

O'Neal, E. C., & Kaufman, L. (1972). The influence of attack, arousal and information about one's arousal upon interpersonal aggression. *Psychonomic Science, 26,* 211–214.

Oring, E. (1984). *Humor and the individual.* Los Angeles: California Folklore Society.

Orlick, T. D. (1981). Positive socialization via cooperative games. *Developmental Psychology, 17,* 426–429.

Osgood, C. E. (1962). *An alternative to war or surrender.* Urbana: University of Illinois Press.

Ostrom, T. M., Steele, C. M., Rosenblood, L. K., & Mirels, H. L. (1971). Modification of delinquent behavior. *Journal of Applied Social Psychology, 1,* 118–136.

Page, M. M., & Scheidt, R. J. (1971). The elusive weapons effect: Demand awareness, evaluation apprehension, and slightly sophisticated subjects. *Journal of Personality and Social Psychology, 20,* 304–318.

Parke, R. D., & Collmer, C. W. (1975). *Child abuse: An interdisciplinary analysis.* Chicago: University of Chicago Press.

Patterson, G. R. (1982). *Coercive family process.* Vol. 3. *A social learning approach.* Eugene, OR: Castalia.

Patterson, G. R., Cobb, J. A., & Ray, R. S. (1973). A social engineering technology for retraining the families of aggressive boys. In H. Adams & I. Unikel (Eds.), *Issues and trends in behavior therapy.* Springfield, IL: Chas. C. Thomas.

Pavlov, I. P. (1927). *Conditioned reflexes.* New York: Oxford University Press.

Payne, D. E., & Payne, K. P. (1970). Newspapers and crime in Detroit. *Journalism Quarterly, 47,* 233–238.

Peeke, H. V. S., Ellman, G. E., & Herz, M. J. (1973). Dose dependent alcohol effects on the aggressive behavior of the convict cichlid (*Cichlasoma nigrofasciatum*). *Behavioral Biology, 8,* 115–122.

Peyreffitte, A. (1982). Paper presented at biennial meeting of International Society for Research on Aggression. Mexico City.

Phillips, D. P. (1983). The impact of mass media violence on U.S. homicides. *American Sociological Review, 48,* 560–568.

Phillips, D. P., & Hensley, J. E. (1984). When violence is rewarded or punished: The impact of mass media stories on homicide. *Journal of Communication, 34,* 101–116.

Piaget, J. (1932). *The moral judgment of the child.* New York: Harcourt, Brace.

Piliavin, I. M., Hardyck, J. A., & Vadum, A. C. (1968). Constraining effects of personal costs on the transgressions of juveniles. *Journal of Personality and Social Psychology, 10,* 227–231.

Pilisuk, M., & Skolnik, P. (1968). Inducing trust: A test of the Osgood proposal. *Journal of Personality and Social Psychology, 8,* 121–133.

Pines, M. P. (1973). An answer to the problem of bail: A proposal in need of empirical confirmation. *Columbia Journal of Law & Social Problems, 9,* 394–441.

Pinkney, A. (1972). *The American way of violence.* New York: Random House.

Plutchik, R., & Kellerman, H. (Eds.). (1980). *Theories of emotion.* New York: Academic Press.

Popper, K. (1959). *The logic of scientific discovery.* New York: Basic Books.

Potegal, M. (1979). The reinforcing value of several types of aggressive behavior: A review. *Aggressive Behavior, 5,* 353–373.

Potegal, M., & Glusman, M. (1983). Effects on muricide of DU27716 injected peripherally or into septum or dorsal raphe. *Aggressive Behavior, 9,* 118.

Powledge, T. (1983, January). Peace pill. *Omni, 5,* 24.

President's Commission on Law Enforcement and Administration of Justice. (1968). *The challenge of crime in a free society.* New York: Avon.

Prisuta, R. H. (1979). Televised sports and political values. *Journal of Communication, 29* (1), 94–102.

Quanty, M. B. (1976). Aggression catharsis. In R. G. Geen & E. C. O'Neal (Eds.), *Perspectives on aggression.* New York: Academic Press.

Quinsey, V. L., Chaplin, T. C., & Carrigan, W. F. (1980). Biofeedback and signaled punishment in the modification of inappropriate sexual age preferences. *Behavior Therapy, 11*, 567–576.

Rapoport, A. (1960). *Fights, games, and debates.* Ann Arbor: University of Michigan Press.

Reik, T. (1962). *Jewish wit.* New York: Gamut.

Rennie, Y. R. (1978). *The search for criminal man.* Lexington, MA: Heath.

Rensberger, B. (1984). What made humans human? *New York Times Magazine,* 8 April.

Rokeach, M. (1973). *The nature of human values.* New York: Free Press.

Rosenbaum, A., & O'Leary, K. D. (1981). Marital violence: Characteristics of abusive couples. *Journal of Consulting and Clinical Psychology, 49,* 63–71.

Rosnow, R. L. (1981). *Paradigms in transition.* New York: Oxford University Press.

Ross, M., Layton, B., Erikson, B., & Schopler, J. (1973). Affect, facial regard, and reactions to crowding. *Journal of Personality and Social Psychology, 28,* 69–76.

Rule, B. G., & Nesdale, A. R. (1976). Emotional arousal and aggressive behavior. *Psychological Bulletin, 83,* 851–863.

Russell, G. W. (1983). Psychological issues in sports aggression. In J. H. Goldstein (Ed.), *Sports violence.* New York: Springer-Verlag.

Sanford, N. (1971). Going beyond prevention. In N. Sanford & C. Comstock (Eds.), *Sanctions for evil.* San Francisco: Jossey-Bass.

Sapolsky, B. S. (1984). Arousal, affect, and the aggression-moderating effect of erotica. In N. Malamuth & E. Donnerstein (Eds.), *Pornography and sexual aggression.* Orlando, FL: Academic Press.

Schanberg, S. H. (1985, January). The Bernhard Goetz mailbag. *New York Times.*

Schmid, A. P., & de Graaf, J. (1982). *Violence as communication: Insurgent terrorism and the western news media.* Beverly Hills, CA: Sage.

Schneirla, T. C. (1968). Instinct and aggression. In A. Montagu (Ed.), *Man and aggression.* New York: Oxford University Press.

Sears, R. R., Maccoby, E. E., & Levin, H. (1957). *Patterns of child-rearing.* Evanston, IL: Row, Peterson.

Segall, M. H. (1983). Aggression in global perspective: A research strategy. In A. P. Goldstein & M. H. Segall (Eds.), *Aggression in global perspective.* New York: Pergamon.

Sellin, T. (1967). Homicides in retentionist and abolitionist states. In T. Sellin (Ed.), *Capital punishment*. New York: Harper & Row.

Shotland, R. L., & Goodstein, L. I. (1984). The role of bystanders in crime control. *Journal of Social Issues, 40* (1), 9–26.

Shuntich, R. J., & Taylor, S. P. (1972). The effects of alcohol on human physical aggression. *Journal of Experimental Research in Personality, 6*, 34–38.

Shupe, L. M. (1954). Alcohol and crime: A study of the urine-alcohol concentration found in 882 persons arrested during or immediately after the commission of a felony. *Journal of Criminal Law & Criminology, 44*, 661–664.

Shure, E. M. (1969). *Our criminal society: The social and legal sources of crime in America* (3rd ed., 1984). Englewood Cliffs, NJ: Prentice-Hall.

Siann, G. (1985). *Accounting for aggression*. London: Allen & Unwin.

Singer, E., Blane, H. T., & Kasschau, R. (1964). Alcoholism and social isolation. *Journal of Abnormal and Social Psychology, 69*, 681–685.

Sipes, R. G. (1973). War, sports and aggression: An empirical test of two rival theories. *American Anthropologist, 75*, 64–86.

Sivak, M. (1983). Society's aggression level as a predictor of traffic fatality rate. *Journal of Safety Research, 14* (3), 93–99.

Smith, M. D. (1979). Social determinants of violence in hockey: A review. *Canadian Journal of Applied Sport Sciences, 4*, 76–82.

Smith, M. D. (1983). What is sports violence? A sociolegal perspective. In J. H. Goldstein (Ed.), *Sports violence*. New York: Springer-Verlag.

Smith, S. B. (1985, January). Why TV won't let up on violence. *New York Times*.

Spinetta, J. J., & Rigler, D. (1972). The child-abusing parent: A psychological review. *Psychological Bulletin, 77*, 296–304.

Stachnik, T. J. (1972). The case against criminal penalties for illicit drug use. *American Psychologist, 27*, 637–642.

Starr, R. (1985, January). Crime: How it destroys, what can be done. *New York Times Magazine*, 19ff.

Staub, E. (1971). The learning and unlearning of aggression: The role of anxiety, empathy, efficacy, and prosocial values. In J. L. Singer (Ed.), *The control of aggression and violence*. New York: Academic Press.

Staub, E. (1975). *The development of prosocial behavior in children*. Morristown, NJ: General Learning Press.

Staub, E., Bar-Tal, D., Karylowski, J., & Reykowski, J. (Eds.),

(1984). *Development and maintenance of prosocial behavior.* New York: Plenum.

Steadman, H. J., & Felson, R. B. (1984). Self-reports of violence. *Criminology, 22,* 321–342.

Steele, B. F., & Pollock, C. B. (1968). A psychiatric study of parents who abuse infants and small children. In R. E. Helfer & C. H. Kempe (Eds.), *The battered child.* Chicago: University of Chicago Press.

Stepansky, P. (1977). *A history of aggression in Freud.* New York: International Universities Press.

Steuer, F. B., Applefield, J. M., & Smith, R. (1971). Televised aggression and the interpersonal aggression of preschool children. *Journal of Experimental Child Psychology, 11,* 442–447.

Storr, A. (1970). *Human aggression.* New York: Bantam.

Straus, M. A., Gelles, R. J., & Steinmetz, S. K. (1979). *Behind closed doors: Violence in the American family.* Garden City, NY: Anchor/Doubleday.

Stumphauzer, J. S. (1972). Increased delay of gratification in young prison inmates through imitation of high-delay peer models. *Journal of Personality and Social Psychology, 21,* 10–17.

Sutherland, E. H. (1949). *White collar crime.* New York: Holt, Rinehart and Winston.

Sutherland, E. H., & Cressey, D. R. (1966). *Principles of criminology* (7th ed.). Philadelphia: Lippincott.

Tanay, E. (1969). Psychiatric study of homicide. *American Journal of Psychiatry, 125,* 1252–1258.

Tannenbaum, P. H. (1971). Studies in film- and television-mediated arousal and aggression: A progress report. In G. Comstock, E. Rubinstein, & J. Murray (Eds.), *Television and social behavior.* Vol. 5. Washington, DC: U.S. Government Printing Office.

Tavris, C. (1982). *Anger: The misunderstood emotion.* New York: Simon & Schuster.

Taylor, S. P., & Leonard, K. E. (1983). Alcohol and human physical aggression. In R. G. Geen & E. I. Donnerstein (Eds.), *Aggression: Theoretical and empirical reviews.* Vol. 2, New York: Academic Press.

Tedeschi, J. T., Smith, R. B., III., & Brown, R. C. Jr. (1974). A reinterpretation of research on aggression. *Psychological Bulletin, 81,* 540–563.

Teplin, L. A. (1984). Criminalizing mental disorder: The comparative arrest rate of the mentally ill. *American Psychologist, 39,* 794–803.

Tinbergen, N. (1951). *The study of instinct.* Oxford: Clarendon.

Tinklenberg, J. R., & Stillman, R. C. (1970). Drug use and violence. In D. N. Daniels, M. F. Gilula, & F. M. Ochberg (Eds.),
Violence and the struggle for existence. Boston: Little, Brown.

Tittle, C. R. (1969). Crime rates and legal sanctions. *Social Problems, 16,* 409–423.

Turner, C. W., Simons, L. S., Berkowitz, L., & Frodi, A. (1977).
The stimulating and inhibiting effects of weapons on aggressive
behavior. *Aggressive Behavior, 3,* 355–378.

U.S. Department of Justice (1983). *Report to the nation on crime
and justice: The data*. Washington, DC: U.S. Government Printing Office.

Van den Haag, E., & Conrad, J. P. (1983). *The death penalty*.
New York: Plenum.

Varela, J. (1970). *Psychological solutions to social problems*. New
York: Academic Press.

Walters, R. H., & Demkow, L. (1963). Timing of punishment as a
determinant of response inhibition. *Child Development, 34,* 207–
214.

Watson, P. (1973, January). More "sane" murders. (London)
Sunday Times.

Watson, R. I., Jr. (1973). Investigation into deindividuation using
a cross-cultural survey technique. *Journal of Personality and
Social Psychology, 25,* 342–345.

Wertham, F. (1969). *A sign for Cain*. New York: Warner.

White, R. K. (1985). *Fearful warriors: A psychological profile of
U.S.-Soviet relations*. New York: Macmillan.

Williams, J., Dunning, E., & Murphy, P. (1984). *Hooligans abroad:
The behavior of English soccer fans at Continental matches*.
London: Routledge & Kegan Paul.

Wilson, E. O. (1975). *Sociobiology*. Cambridge, MA: Harvard
University Press.

Wilson, J. (1973). *A teacher's guide to moral education*. London:
Geoffrey Chapman.

Wilson, J. Q., & Herrostein, R. J. (1985). *Crime and human nature*.
New York: Simon & Schuster.

Witkin, H. A., Mednick, S. A., Shulsinger, F., Bakkestrom, E.,
Christiansen, K. O., Goodenough, D. R., Hirschhorn, K., Lund-
steen, C., Owen, D. R., Philip, J., Rubin, D. B, & Stocking, M.
(1976). Criminality in XYY and XXY men. *Science, 193,* 547–
555.

Wolfe, B. M., & Baron, R. A. (1971). Laboratory aggression related to aggression in naturalistic social situations: Effects of an
aggressive model on the behavior of college students and prisoner
observers. *Psychonomic Science, 24,* 193–194.

Wolfgang, M. E. (1958). *Patterns in criminal homicide.* Philadelphia: University of Pennsylvania Press.

Wolfgang, M. E., & Ferracuti, F. (1967). *The subculture of violence.* London: Tavistock.

Wolfgang, M. E., Figlio, R., & Sellin, T. (1972). *Delinquency in a birth cohort.* Chicago: University of Chicago Press.

Yaeger, R. C. (1979). *Seasons of shame.* New York: McGraw-Hill.

Yancey, W. L. (1972). Architecture, interaction, and social control: The case of a large scale housing project. In J. Wohlwill & D. Carson (Eds.), *Environment and the social sciences.* Washington, DC: American Psychological Association.

Yarrow, M. R., Campbell, J. D., & Burton, R. V. (1968). *Child rearing: An inquiry into research and methods.* San Francisco: Jossey-Bass.

Zajonc, R. B. (1980). Feeling and thinking: Preferences need no inferences. *American Psychologist, 35,* 151–175.

Zillmann, D. (1971). Excitation transfer in communication-mediated aggressive behavior. *Journal of Experimental Social Psychology, 7,* 419–434.

Zillmann, D. (1979). *Hostility and aggression.* Hillsdale, NJ: Lawrence Erlbaum Associates.

Zillmann, D. (1983). Disparagement humor. In P. E. McGhee & J. H. Goldstein (Eds.), *Handbook of humor research.* Vol. 1. *Basic issues.* New York: Springer-Verlag.

Zillmann, D. (1984). *Connections between sex and aggression.* Hillsdale, NJ: Lawrence Erlbaum Associates.

Zillmann, D., Bryant, J., & Sapolsky, B. S. (1979). The enjoyment of watching sports contests. In J. H. Goldstein (Ed.), *Sports, games, and play.* Hillsdale, NJ: Lawrence Erlbaum Associates.

Zimbardo, P. G. (1969). The human choice: Individuation, reason and order versus deindividuation, impulse and chaos. In W. J. Arnold & D. Levine (Eds.), *Nebraska symposium on motivation.* Lincoln: University of Nebraska Press.

Zinberg, N. E., & Fellman, G. A. (1967). Violence: Biological need and social control. *Social Forces, 45,* 533–541.

Name Index

Subject Index